NUREMBERG TRAVEL GUIDE 2025

EXPLORING HISTORY, CULTURE, AND HIDDEN GEMS IN BAVARIA'S TIMELESS CITY

MAYA WESTBROOK

4

TABLE OF CONTENTS

Welcome to Nuremberg, a city where history, innovation, and charm blend seamlessly to offer an unforgettable experience. Located in the heart of Bavaria, Nuremberg is celebrated for its medieval architecture, rich cultural heritage, and vibrant modern lifestyle. Whether you're a first-time visitor or a returning traveler, Nuremberg promises an adventure that combines historic intrigue with contemporary allure.

Step Back in Time

Nuremberg has preserved its history with remarkable care. As you wander through the Old Town, you'll encounter cobblestone streets, half-timbered houses, and the formidable Nuremberg Castle. Here, echoes of the past—medieval markets, imperial landmarks, and intricate Gothic churches—come alive. History enthusiasts will find endless fascination in exploring sites like the Albrecht Dürer House, the home of the Renaissance painter, and the Documentation Center Nazi Party Rally Grounds, which offers a somber yet vital glimpse into Germany's history during WWII.

Art, Culture, and Innovation

1.2 BRIEF HISTORY OF NUREMBERG

Nuremberg, known for its rich medieval history and cultural heritage, is a city that has evolved through significant phases since its establishment in the 11th century. Founded around 1050, the city grew rapidly, thanks to its strategic location on key trade routes. By the 13th century, Nuremberg was recognized as an Imperial Free City of the Holy Roman Empire, granting it autonomy and elevating its status in

Europe. This period sparked a golden era, and the city became a center for commerce, artistry, and intellectual growth, drawing skilled craftsmen, artists, and scholars from all over Europe.

The 15th and 16th centuries marked the height of Nuremberg's prosperity, driven by its thriving trade and innovations in art and science. This was also the era when famed artists like Albrecht Dürer, a Renaissance master, flourished in the city. The spirit of invention thrived with figures like Johannes Regiomontanus and Peter Henlein, the latter credited with creating the first portable watch. Nuremberg's architectural achievements also flourished, with Gothic churches and elaborate fortifications transforming the city's skyline.

The Reformation, sparked by Martin Luther in 1517, reached Nuremberg swiftly. The city embraced Lutheranism in 1525, which led to significant religious and political changes. However, Nuremberg's fortunes declined during the Thirty Years' War (1618-1648), which ravaged much of Central Europe, leading to economic struggles and a slow recovery.

In the 19th century, Nuremberg saw a resurgence with industrialization. The arrival of the first German railway in 1835 between Nuremberg and nearby Fürth was a milestone that positioned the city as a modern industrial hub. This era also preserved its historical architecture, with some restoration projects blending modern industry with traditional Bavarian culture.

Nuremberg's role in the 20th century is marked by its connection to the Nazi regime, which used the city as a rallying point for propaganda and ideology. The infamous Nuremberg Rallies were held here in the 1930s, leaving a complex legacy. World War II heavily damaged the city, but a dedicated post-war restoration project helped rebuild Nuremberg, restoring many of its medieval structures and monuments.

In 1945-1946, Nuremberg hosted the landmark Nuremberg Trials, where Nazi war criminals were prosecuted, underscoring the city's role in global justice and human rights history. Today, Nuremberg balances its historical legacy with modern vibrancy. Its well-preserved medieval architecture, cultural institutions, and bustling markets draw visitors worldwide, offering a deep dive into both the past and present of German history.

centuries-old architectural craftsmanship. Visitors can wander through the Altstadt (Old Town), encircled by historic walls and dotted with half-timbered houses, Gothic churches, and cobblestone streets that speak of its medieval past. Key landmarks like St. Lorenz Church and the beautiful Hauptmarkt square, where the famed Schöner Brunnen fountain stands, are perfect stops for anyone seeking authentic, picturesque settings.

2. History Brought to Life

Nuremberg holds a significant place in world history, offering travelers a deeply insightful perspective. As the location of the infamous Nuremberg Trials and Nazi party rallies, the city provides opportunities to learn about this dark chapter through sites like the Documentation Center Nazi Party Rally Grounds. Additionally, the Memorium Nuremberg Trials allows visitors to understand this pivotal moment in post-World War II history. For those interested in medieval history, the Nuremberg Castle and the Germanisches Nationalmuseum house artifacts that tell the story of the city's role in the Holy Roman Empire and as a center of Renaissance art and innovation.

3. A Hub of German Art and Culture

Nuremberg is home to a thriving arts scene, offering visitors everything from traditional German craftsmanship to contemporary art. The city proudly honors the legacy of Albrecht Dürer, the Renaissance painter and printmaker, whose former home now serves as a museum. Art lovers can immerse themselves in Dürer's work and explore exhibitions at the Neues Museum, a modern art museum that bridges the city's past with contemporary culture. In 2025,

Nuremberg will host various art events and festivals, allowing travelers to witness the lively spirit of Bavarian culture and creativity.

4. Culinary Delights and Local Breweries

No visit to Nuremberg is complete without savoring its famous local flavors. The city's culinary scene is deeply rooted in Franconian traditions, featuring delicious specialties like Nuremberg bratwurst and lebkuchen (gingerbread), which has been a staple since medieval times. The city is dotted with cozy beer halls and traditional restaurants, where visitors can enjoy hearty German fare alongside locally brewed Franconian beer. For beer enthusiasts, Nuremberg's beer culture is a must-experience, with many historic breweries offering tours and tastings, showcasing the region's unique brewing heritage.

5. Seasonal Festivals and Events

In 2025, Nuremberg will host a range of festivals and events that showcase its vibrant traditions and modern charm. The city's iconic Christkindlesmarkt, one of the world's oldest and most famous Christmas markets, draws visitors from around the globe with its festive stalls, holiday treats, and traditional crafts. In the warmer months, events like the Altstadtfest (Old Town Festival) and Bardentreffen, an international music festival, fill the city with music, food, and celebration, offering travelers a chance to connect with the local culture. Seasonal events are a great reason to visit Nuremberg at any time of the year, providing an opportunity to experience the city's friendly and welcoming atmosphere.

6. A Gateway to the Franconian Countryside

connect Nuremberg with popular holiday destinations, adding more flexibility for those planning a trip.

Facilities and Services

Nuremberg Airport provides a comfortable, modern experience with amenities designed to meet traveler needs. Key features include:

- **Dining and Shopping:** Enjoy a variety of cafes, bakeries, and restaurants before or after your flight, with options for quick bites or a sit-down meal. Duty-free shopping offers a range of products, from local souvenirs to high-end cosmetics and liquor.

- **Wi-Fi and Business Services:**

Free Wi-Fi is available throughout the airport, and there are workspaces for business travelers. Additionally, several charging stations ensure your devices stay powered up.

- **Lounges:**

your accommodation in advance, as this can be a comfortable, budget-friendly alternative.

Tips for Arrivals and Departures

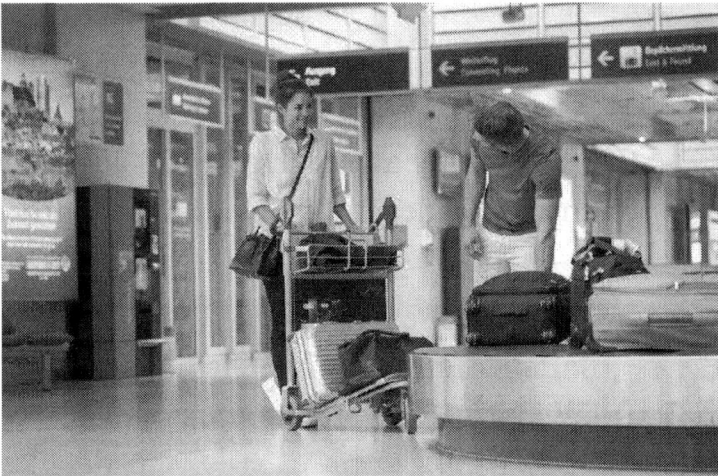

- **Peak Times:** Nuremberg Airport sees more traffic in summer and around major events like Christmas markets, so plan ahead during these periods.

- **Immigration and Security:** Nuremberg is part of the Schengen Zone, which simplifies entry for most European travelers. Non-Schengen travelers should be prepared for passport control. The airport is known for efficient processing, but allow extra time if traveling during peak seasons.

Accessibility

Nuremberg Airport is accessible and accommodating to travelers with limited mobility. Elevators, ramps, and assistance

Arriving in Nuremberg by Train

International and Long-Distance Trains:

Nuremberg Hauptbahnhof (Nuremberg Central Station) is a major hub on Germany's high-speed ICE (InterCity Express) network, providing direct routes from cities like Berlin, Munich, Frankfurt, and Hamburg. International travelers can also reach Nuremberg easily, with trains connecting from Vienna, Prague, Zurich, and other European cities. The ICE trains offer fast and comfortable journeys, making it possible to reach Nuremberg from Munich in just over an hour, Frankfurt in about two hours, and Berlin in roughly three hours.

Regional Connections:
If you're already in Bavaria or a nearby region, Nuremberg is accessible via regional trains (RE and RB). These are slightly slower than the ICE or IC (InterCity) trains but are often more affordable, especially if you're exploring nearby towns or smaller cities. Trains to Nuremberg from places like Bamberg, Würzburg, and Regensburg are frequent and reliable.

Tickets and Deals:
Deutsche Bahn offers a variety of ticket options that can help you save money, depending on your travel plans. For instance:

- **Bayern Ticket**:

This ticket is an excellent choice if you plan to travel within Bavaria. Available for single travelers or groups, it provides unlimited travel on regional trains and public transportation in Nuremberg for a day. Valid after 9 a.m. on weekdays and all day on weekends, it's an economical option for families or groups.

- **Saver Fares:** If you book in advance, you may find discounted fares on ICE and IC routes. These Saver Tickets offer substantial savings but are limited in availability, so booking early is advisable.

- **Deutschland Ticket (Germany Ticket):**

This nationwide ticket allows unlimited travel on local and regional trains across Germany for a flat monthly rate. Perfect for those planning an extended stay and frequent regional travel.

Navigating Nuremberg by Train

Nuremberg Hauptbahnhof (Central Station):

The central station is a landmark in its own right, with a mix of historic architecture and modern amenities. Located near the old town (Altstadt), it serves as a gateway to Nuremberg's main attractions. Inside the station, you'll find everything you need, including ticket counters, automated machines, luggage storage, food options, and tourist information. From here, it's a short walk to Nuremberg's historic sites like the Imperial Castle, Hauptmarkt (Central Market), and St. Lorenz Church.

Public Transport Integration:

Nuremberg has an integrated public transportation system, and your train ticket often includes travel on local trams, buses, and the U-Bahn (subway). The U-Bahn lines U1, U2, and U3 connect the train station to various parts of the city, making it easy to reach nearby districts or attractions. The tram lines 4, 5, 6, 7, 8, and 9 also stop near the station, offering another convenient option for getting around.

Day Trips from Nuremberg by Train

One of the best aspects of basing yourself in Nuremberg is the array of nearby destinations accessible by train. Here are a few popular day trips:

- **Bamberg:**

Known for its medieval architecture and unique smoked beer, Bamberg is a UNESCO World Heritage site reachable in under an hour.

- **Rothenburg ob der Tauber:**

This quintessential German town, famed for its preserved medieval walls and picturesque scenery, is around an hour and a half by regional train.

- **Regensburg:**

Another UNESCO-listed city with Roman roots, Regensburg offers a charming old town and is about an hour and a half by train.

- **Munich:**

If you're interested in Bavarian culture and history, Munich is a short journey by ICE, making it ideal for a day visit.

Tips for Train Travel in Nuremberg

- **Plan Ahead:**

Trains in Germany are generally punctual, so be at the platform a few minutes before departure. Check the DB app or website for real-time schedules and platform information.

- **Luggage and Accessibility:**

Most trains, especially ICE trains, have ample luggage space and accessible facilities for those with mobility needs. However, if you have large bags, arriving early to secure space can be beneficial.

- **Enjoy the Scenery:**

Many routes around Bavaria offer scenic views of countryside, forests, and villages. Window seats are worth reserving, especially if you're traveling on routes through the Franconian or Bavarian landscapes.

2.3 BY CAR

Nuremberg is a fantastic city to explore by car, offering flexibility to uncover both its iconic landmarks and hidden gems at your own pace. Driving here can be enjoyable, especially as it allows access to nearby regions in Franconia and Bavaria for day trips. However, there are a few tips and tricks to make your journey smoother and stress-free.

1. Driving in Nuremberg's Historic Center

- **Limited Car Access:** The Altstadt, or Old Town, is a pedestrian-friendly zone with limited access for cars to preserve its historic charm. Streets are often cobbled and narrow, which can make driving challenging. Parking is generally restricted here, so visitors are encouraged to use nearby parking facilities and then explore on foot.

- **Traffic Regulations:**

Keep in mind that Germany has strict traffic rules, especially in urban areas. Speed limits within the city are usually 50 km/h unless otherwise posted, while in school or residential areas, they may drop to 30 km/h. Obey all signs, as traffic cameras are common.

2. Parking in Nuremberg

- **Public Parking Garages:** Nuremberg has numerous multi-story parking garages located conveniently around the city center. These garages often charge hourly or daily rates, typically ranging from €2–€5 per hour. Popular options include the Parkhaus Hauptmarkt and the Parkhaus Sterntor, both close to central attractions.

- **Park & Ride (P+R):**

To avoid city traffic, consider using Nuremberg's P+R system. These parking lots are located on the outskirts and connected to public transit, allowing you to park your car inexpensively and take the U-Bahn (subway) or bus directly into the city.

- **Street Parking:**

Paid street parking is available in some areas, especially outside the city center. However, it can be limited and sometimes difficult to find a spot, particularly on weekends or during events. Be sure to pay for your ticket at nearby machines and display it on your dashboard.

3. Driving on the Autobahn to Nuremberg

- **Efficient Access:**

Nuremberg is connected by several major autobahns, making it an easy drive from nearby German cities like Munich, Stuttgart, and Frankfurt. Autobahns A3, A6, and A9 serve the region well, providing direct routes to and from the city.

- **Speed Limits and Rules:**

While parts of the autobahn have no speed limits, many sections around cities do impose speed restrictions. Be mindful of posted speed limits and remember that Germany enforces right-lane driving except when passing. Also, it's wise to observe the "recommended" speed limit of 130 km/h, especially when traffic is moderate to heavy.

4. Toll Information

- For standard vehicles, there are generally no tolls on Germany's highways or city roads. However, keep in mind that Germany requires an emissions sticker (Umweltplakette) for driving in certain "low-emission" zones. Nuremberg has such zones, and these stickers are usually available at car rental agencies or for purchase online if you're bringing your own vehicle.

5. Car Rentals in Nuremberg

- **Availability:**

Car rentals are easily accessible in Nuremberg, with agencies located at the airport, main train station (Hauptbahnhof), and various city locations. International companies like Hertz, Sixt, and Europcar have branches here, as well as local options.

- **Requirements:** To rent a car, you typically need a valid driver's license, passport, and a credit card. For non-EU travelers, an International Driving Permit (IDP) is often recommended but not always required. Renters must usually be at least 21 years old, and surcharges may apply for drivers under 25.

6. Day Trips by Car from Nuremberg

- Having a car allows for easy day trips to nearby attractions. Nuremberg's location in Bavaria is ideal for excursions to the medieval town of Rothenburg ob der Tauber, the castle-laden Franconian Switzerland region, and the beautiful cities of Bamberg and Regensburg, each within a 1- to 2-hour drive.

- **Planning Your Route:**

German highways are generally well-marked, and GPS or mobile navigation apps are commonly used. Plan your routes in advance to avoid unexpected toll roads or traffic, and check for any roadwork updates, as summer months can see more construction projects on highways.

7. Tips for a Smooth Driving Experience

- **Fuel Stations**:

Gas stations are plentiful along highways and within the city. While gas prices may vary, highway stops tend to be more expensive, so fueling up in town may save a few euros.

- **Eco-Friendly Zones:** Make sure your rental car has the proper emissions sticker if you plan to drive into low-emission zones. Most rental cars in Germany come equipped with these, but double-check with the rental agency if you plan to visit multiple cities.

- **Winter Driving:**

If visiting in winter, check that your rental vehicle has winter tires. These are mandatory during snowy or icy conditions, as Germany enforces strict road safety laws.

2.4 PUBLIC TRANSPORT OPTIONS

Nuremberg's public transportation system is one of Germany's most efficient, making it easy for tourists to navigate the city and surrounding areas. The city has a well-integrated system that includes trams, buses, and U-Bahn (subway) and S-Bahn (regional trains), all operated by VAG Nürnberg (Verkehrs-Aktiengesellschaft Nürnberg). Here's a detailed look at the main options available.

U-Bahn (Subway)

The U-Bahn system in Nuremberg consists of three lines (U1, U2, and U3) covering a range of city destinations, including central hubs, residential areas, and popular tourist sites.

- **Line U1** connects the city center with eastern and western suburbs, making it ideal for reaching places like the Nuremberg Exhibition Center.

- **Line U2** runs directly from the airport to the central railway station and the heart of the city, providing a quick, straightforward option for travelers arriving by plane.

- **Line U3** is an automatic line that connects areas in the north and south of Nuremberg.

The U-Bahn operates frequently, with trains arriving approximately every 5 to 10 minutes during peak hours. Services run from around 4 a.m. to midnight, with night buses available to cover areas once the U-Bahn stops operating.

S-Bahn (Suburban Trains)

The S-Bahn system connects Nuremberg with nearby towns and cities, like Erlangen, Fürth, and Bamberg. With four lines (S1 to S4), the S-Bahn is particularly useful for those looking to explore beyond Nuremberg.

- **S1** is popular for travelers heading to Bamberg and other scenic towns.

- **S2** covers the route from Nuremberg through Erlangen and Roth, making it useful for university areas and residential neighborhoods.

The S-Bahn services run less frequently than the U-Bahn but are well-coordinated with other modes of transportation to offer smooth transfers. Tickets for the S-Bahn are integrated with the Nuremberg public transport system, allowing easy transfers with a single ticket.

Trams

Nuremberg's tram network is well-distributed across the city and is especially useful for reaching neighborhoods that might be less accessible by U-Bahn or S-Bahn. The tram lines are marked from 4 to 9 and serve routes that intersect with U-Bahn and bus lines, providing comprehensive city coverage.

Trams are a convenient option for exploring some of Nuremberg's historic neighborhoods, as they stop at major tourist attractions like the St. Lawrence Church and Germanisches Nationalmuseum. Trams typically operate from 5 a.m. until midnight, with frequencies of around 10 minutes during busy periods.

Buses

Buses are an essential part of Nuremberg's transport network, covering areas not accessible by other forms of public transit. With a wide-reaching network, buses connect the suburbs and city outskirts to central Nuremberg and are especially useful for accessing specific sites not on tram or U-Bahn routes.

Night buses operate after the U-Bahn, S-Bahn, and trams stop, offering routes that cover main areas until the early morning hours. This is particularly helpful for night travelers or those looking to enjoy Nuremberg's nightlife.

Ticketing and Pass Options

Nuremberg's public transport system operates on a zone-based ticketing system, making it easy to buy the correct fare. Tickets can be purchased at U-Bahn stations, on trams and buses, or through the VAG mobile app.

- **Single Tickets:** Useful for short trips, these tickets allow travel within one or more zones.

- **Day Passes:** Ideal for tourists, these offer unlimited travel within Nuremberg for one day. Group day tickets are also available, making it cost-effective for families or groups.

- **Weekly and Monthly Passes:** Suitable for longer stays, these passes allow unlimited travel and can be purchased based on the zones needed.

It's important to validate your ticket before boarding to avoid fines. For digital tickets purchased through the app, validation is automatic upon purchase.

Tips for Tourists

- **Nürnberg Card:**

This card grants free access to public transport and admission to many museums and attractions. It's a great value for tourists planning to explore the city extensively.

- **Plan Ahead:**

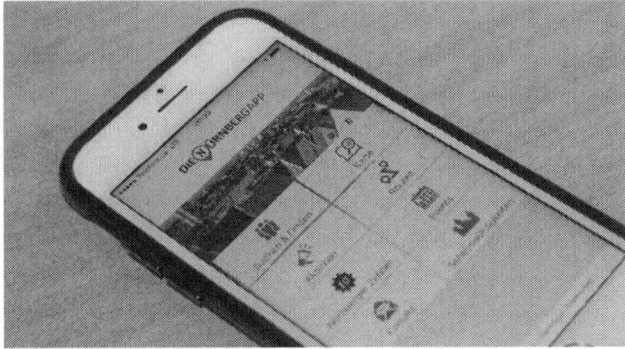

The VAG Nürnberg website and app provide real-time schedules, maps, and trip planning tools, helping you to choose the quickest routes and check live updates.

Accessibility

Nuremberg's public transport system is generally accessible, with elevators and ramps at most U-Bahn and S-Bahn stations, as well as low-floor trams and buses. Most stations have visual and auditory signals to assist passengers with disabilities.

3.0 WHERE TO STAY

3.1 OVERVIEW OF ACCOMMODATION OPTIONS

Nuremberg offers a diverse range of accommodations that cater to every type of traveler, whether you're here for the historic sites, a Christmas market getaway, or a business trip. The city has options to fit various budgets, preferences, and styles, making it easy to find the perfect place to unwind after a day of exploration.

1. Luxury Hotels

Nuremberg is home to several high-end hotels, often located near the Old Town or by the city's most iconic landmarks. These accommodations offer top-tier services, elegant rooms, and a range of amenities such as spas, gourmet restaurants, and concierge services. Luxury hotels often have beautifully preserved historical architecture blended with modern comforts, providing guests a taste of both history and indulgence. The area around the castle and along Königstraße offers some of the city's most luxurious stays, ideal for travelers who want to immerse themselves in Nuremberg's elegance.

2. Mid-Range Hotels and Boutique Stays

For travelers seeking comfort without a steep price tag, Nuremberg has a wide selection of mid-range hotels and boutique accommodations. Many of these are situated within walking distance of Old Town's main attractions, providing easy access to the city's best restaurants, shopping spots, and historical sites. Boutique hotels often bring a personal touch, with unique decor and local themes that reflect Nuremberg's culture. These options typically offer amenities such as breakfast, Wi-Fi, and convenient public transport access, making them a practical choice for families, couples, or solo travelers.

3. Budget Hotels and Hostels

Budget-conscious travelers will find several affordable hotels and hostels around Nuremberg that don't skimp on comfort or convenience. Most budget accommodations are modern, clean, and centrally located, ensuring guests are well-connected to public transit and major attractions. Hostels, in particular, offer a friendly, social atmosphere, with many providing communal areas, shared kitchens, and organized events. This option is perfect for young travelers, backpackers, and anyone looking to meet fellow explorers on their journey.

4. Apartments and Vacation Rentals

For those who prefer a home-away-from-home experience, Nuremberg has a wide array of vacation rentals and serviced apartments. Ideal for families or long-term visitors, these rentals provide a cozy and private space with full kitchens and multiple bedrooms. Many are located in residential areas, offering an authentic experience of daily life in Nuremberg. Vacation rentals can vary from modern apartments to charming historic flats, making it easy to find one that fits your travel style.

5. Unique Stays

If you're looking for something memorable, Nuremberg also has unique lodging options that can make your stay even more special. Some hotels are set within medieval buildings, allowing guests to experience the history of Nuremberg in an immersive way. Other unique stays include eco-friendly accommodations, art-themed hotels, and even converted castles. Staying in one of these places can add an extra layer of charm to your Nuremberg experience, making it feel like more than just a place to sleep.

3.2 RECOMMENDED HOTELS

Nuremberg offers a wide range of accommodations to suit different budgets and preferences, from historic luxury hotels in the heart of the city to cozy boutique options and budget-friendly stays. Here's a list of some top recommendations for every type of traveler:

1. Hotel Drei Raben

Location: Altstadt (Old Town)

Description: Hotel Drei Raben, or "Three Ravens," is a boutique hotel located in the heart of Nuremberg's Old Town. Known for its unique storytelling concept, each room tells a local legend, blending historic charm with modern comfort. Guests often praise the attention to detail, friendly service, and themed décor. Its prime location near the central market square and landmarks like St. Lorenz Church makes it a great choice for sightseeing.

2. Le Méridien Grand Hotel

Location: Near Hauptbahnhof (Central Station)
Description: For travelers seeking classic luxury, Le Méridien Grand Hotel offers a taste of elegance with a rich history. The hotel features opulent interiors with marble floors, grand staircases, and chandeliers, exuding old-world charm. Its rooms are spacious and comfortable, with modern amenities for a premium stay. Guests appreciate the proximity to the train

station, making it ideal for those arriving by rail, and it's a short walk to Old Town.

3. Park Plaza Nuremberg

Location: Near Hauptbahnhof
Description: A contemporary option for modern travelers, Park Plaza combines stylish design with a welcoming atmosphere. The hotel's amenities include a fitness center, an on-site restaurant serving international cuisine, and comfortable, well-appointed rooms. Located

across from the Central Station, it's convenient for both business and leisure travelers and within walking distance of the city's main attractions.

4. Hotel Victoria

Location: Next to Königstor (King's Gate)
Description: Hotel Victoria is a charming, family-run hotel with over a century of history. It blends tradition with modern comfort, and many rooms offer views of the city walls and historic architecture. Guests love the cozy atmosphere, friendly staff, and unique location next to the

ancient Königstor, which offers immediate access to the Old Town. Hotel Victoria also has a reputation for its excellent breakfast buffet featuring fresh, local ingredients.

5. Novotel Nuremberg Centre Ville

Location: Near Central Station
Description: This modern and family-friendly hotel is part of the reliable Novotel chain, providing a balance of affordability and quality. With spacious rooms, an indoor swimming pool,

and a children's play area, it's particularly popular among families. The hotel's central location makes it easy to explore the city on foot or by public transport, while amenities like a sauna and fitness center add extra comfort.

6. Adina Apartment Hotel Nuremberg

Location: Near Germanisches Nationalmuseum
Description: Adina Apartment Hotel is ideal for travelers who prefer apartment-style accommodations with the flexibility of self-catering. Each suite is equipped with a

kitchenette, living area, and laundry facilities, offering a home-away-from-home experience. It's popular among longer-stay guests and families. The hotel is close to the Germanisches Nationalmuseum and a short walk from Nuremberg's top attractions.

7. Motel One Nuremberg-City

Location: Near Central Station
Description: For budget-conscious travelers who don't want to compromise on style, Motel One offers affordable, minimalist rooms with modern design and comfortable furnishings. This hotel is part of a popular German chain

known for its consistent quality and sleek interiors. While basic, the rooms have everything you need for a comfortable stay. Guests appreciate the convenient location near the train station and easy access to Nuremberg's sights.

8. Sheraton Carlton Hotel Nuremberg

Location: Near Hauptbahnhof
Description: Another luxurious option near the Central Station, the Sheraton Carlton Hotel offers spacious rooms with elegant décor and a

rooftop spa. Business and leisure travelers alike enjoy the hotel's high-end amenities, which include a wellness center with panoramic city views, a bar, and an on-site restaurant serving regional and international dishes. The proximity to the Old Town and main station makes it highly convenient.

9. Burghotel Nuremberg

Location: Near Imperial Castle (Kaiserburg)
Description: Burghotel is a family-run hotel located close to the Kaiserburg, Nuremberg's

iconic Imperial Castle. This charming hotel provides an intimate experience, offering rooms with views of the castle and the Old Town. It's perfect for travelers interested in Nuremberg's medieval history, with rooms that feature traditional, warm decor. The hotel also has a lovely rooftop terrace where guests can enjoy panoramic views of the city.

10. Acomhotel Nuremberg

Location: Nordostbahnhof (North-East Station)
Description: For those seeking affordable, no-frills accommodations outside the city center, Acomhotel offers good value and easy access to

public transport. The hotel has a contemporary feel with simple yet comfortable rooms, ideal for budget travelers and business visitors. Its location near Nordostbahnhof provides quick connections to the Old Town via the U-Bahn, making it a convenient option for guests who don't mind staying slightly outside the hustle and bustle.

3.3 BUDGET-FRIENDLY HOSTELS

When visiting Nuremberg on a budget, there are a variety of hostels that combine comfort, convenience, and affordability. Here's a look at some top budget-friendly hostels where travelers can save money without sacrificing a great experience.

1. Five Reasons Hostel & Hotel

- **Overview:** Located close to the historic city center, Five Reasons is known for its relaxed atmosphere and modern facilities. It's highly rated for cleanliness, friendly staff, and a central location, making it a popular choice for both solo travelers and groups.

- **Amenities:** The hostel offers mixed dorms, private rooms, free Wi-Fi, a guest kitchen, and a cozy common lounge. The dorms are spacious, with personal lockers, individual reading lights, and privacy curtains, ensuring a comfortable stay.

- **Why It's Budget-Friendly:** Five Reasons provides affordable accommodation without cutting corners on quality or location, offering great value for those looking to experience Nuremberg on a budget.

2. A&O Nuremberg Hauptbahnhof

- **Overview:** Conveniently situated near the main train station, A&O is ideal for travelers who want easy access to transportation. This hostel is part of a reputable budget hotel chain across Europe, so it's known for maintaining consistent standards.

- **Amenities:** A&O Nuremberg offers a variety of rooms from dorms to family rooms, as well as private en-suite rooms. Facilities include free Wi-Fi, a 24-hour front desk, an on-site bar, and a rooftop terrace with panoramic views of the city. They also have bike rentals, perfect for exploring nearby attractions.

- **Why It's Budget-Friendly:** With its range of budget options, from shared dorms to affordable private rooms, A&O allows travelers to pick what best fits their needs. The hostel also often runs discounts for extended stays, making it a good choice for budget-conscious tourists planning a longer visit.

3. Hostel Nürnberg

- **Overview:** For a more local experience, Hostel Nürnberg offers a laid-back and intimate vibe. Located near the iconic Kaiserburg Castle, this hostel is close to several popular landmarks, so guests are within walking distance of many must-see sites.

- **Amenities:** It has a mix of dormitory-style rooms and private options, a shared kitchen, and communal areas for mingling with other travelers. Guests appreciate the personal touch provided by the staff and the homelike feel of the place.

- **Why It's Budget-Friendly:** Hostel Nürnberg is known for its simple but comfortable accommodations at reasonable rates. Its proximity to key sites eliminates the need for extra transportation costs, helping visitors save even more.

4. City Hostel Nürnberg

- **Overview:** This hostel offers straightforward, comfortable lodging with a no-frills approach. It's centrally located, ideal for those looking to explore the Altstadt (Old Town) without straying far from the main attractions.

- **Amenities:** City Hostel Nürnberg provides basic dorms and private rooms, a communal kitchen, and a small lounge area. They focus on keeping costs low while offering essentials like free Wi-Fi and luggage storage.

- **Why It's Budget-Friendly:** With its minimalist approach and affordable rates, City Hostel Nürnberg attracts budget travelers who are primarily interested in a clean, comfortable place to sleep. Its location in the heart of the city means that major sites, restaurants, and public transport are all within easy reach.

5. Jugendherberge Nürnberg (Nuremberg Youth Hostel)

- **Overview:** Located in a historic building just below Nuremberg Castle, Jugendherberge Nürnberg is one of the oldest youth hostels in the city, making it an interesting and authentic option for history enthusiasts.

- **Amenities:** The hostel has both dormitories and private rooms, a daily breakfast buffet, and a café where guests can unwind after a day of exploring. Other facilities include a library, meeting rooms, and outdoor seating areas, making it a great choice for solo travelers, families, and groups.

- **Why It's Budget-Friendly:** Jugendherberge Nürnberg offers all-inclusive rates that cover essentials like breakfast and linens, which keeps additional costs low. It also provides family rooms, making it an excellent option for budget-conscious families visiting the city.

6. The Keep Hostel

- **Overview:** Situated close to the Old Town, The Keep Hostel focuses on offering a modern, stylish hostel experience while staying budget-friendly. Its bright interiors and clean design make it particularly appealing to younger travelers.

- **Amenities:** Dormitories with cozy beds, shared and private bathrooms, lockers, free Wi-Fi, and a social area are just some of the amenities guests can enjoy. The common lounge is a popular spot for socializing, often with events or gatherings organized by the hostel.

- **Why It's Budget-Friendly:** The Keep Hostel's affordable dorm rates make it a favorite among backpackers and budget-conscious solo travelers. With its inviting atmosphere and location, it's an excellent choice for those looking to meet fellow travelers while exploring Nuremberg on a budget.

3.4 UNIQUE STAYS (AIRBNBS, GUESTHOUSES)

Nuremberg offers a range of unique accommodations, blending historical charm with modern comforts, perfect for travelers seeking something out of the ordinary. Whether you're drawn to medieval architecture, cozy spaces, or urban chic, here are some of the best Airbnbs and guesthouses that capture the city's distinctive character.

1. Historic Altstadt Apartment

For a true taste of Nuremberg's history, consider a stay in a beautifully restored apartment within the Altstadt, the city's old town. These rentals often feature exposed timber beams, rustic decor, and views of cobbled streets, giving a glimpse into the city's medieval past. Many of these apartments come with modern amenities like free Wi-Fi, smart TVs, and fully equipped kitchens while preserving an old-world charm that feels like stepping back in time. This is an excellent choice for travelers who appreciate both history and comfort.

2. The Half-Timbered Guesthouse

Nestled in one of Nuremberg's quaint neighborhoods, the half-timbered guesthouses offer an idyllic, storybook setting. These homes are instantly recognizable for their wooden framework exterior and cozy interiors with slanted roofs and antique furnishings. Perfect for couples or small groups, these guesthouses often provide a cozy, intimate experience while still being close to the city center. Some properties may even include small gardens or patios, ideal for sipping morning coffee or an evening glass of Franconian wine.

3. The Art Loft

For lovers of modern design, an Art Loft in the heart of Nuremberg offers a vibrant yet sophisticated place to stay. These lofts are typically decorated with local artwork, blending industrial design with colorful, contemporary decor. They often come equipped with open-plan kitchens, spacious living areas, and high ceilings. Located near the city's art galleries, shops, and cafes, an Art Loft is a perfect fit for travelers looking to experience Nuremberg's thriving art scene up close.

4. Riverside Retreats

Nuremberg's riverside is lined with charming properties that overlook the Pegnitz River, offering a tranquil escape in the heart of the city. Staying here means waking up to scenic river views and enjoying easy access to riverside paths for morning strolls or cycling. These Airbnbs and guesthouses often feature large windows, minimalistic decor, and easy access to nature, making them ideal for a relaxing and rejuvenating stay. Some hosts even provide bicycles or kayaks to explore the river at your own pace.

5. The Castle View Apartment

For an unforgettable experience, consider booking a Castle View apartment. These accommodations offer stunning views of the Kaiserburg (Imperial Castle), one of Nuremberg's most iconic landmarks. Imagine having breakfast on a balcony with a direct view of the castle or enjoying the evening lights as they illuminate its ancient walls. These properties blend modern comfort with prime location, allowing you to soak in the city's heritage from the comfort of your private space.

6. Converted Brewery Loft

In the more eclectic parts of Nuremberg, you'll find converted lofts in historic buildings, like old breweries or factories. These unique stays capture the city's industrial past with a stylish twist, offering open-plan spaces, exposed brick walls, and designer furnishings. Many of these lofts are now in trendy neighborhoods, filled with art galleries, craft beer pubs, and artisan shops, making them a favorite among younger travelers and creatives. Staying here provides a taste of Nuremberg's modern, bohemian vibe.

7. Eco-Friendly Guesthouses

Nuremberg is known for its commitment to sustainability, and eco-conscious travelers will find plenty of green accommodations to choose from. These eco-friendly guesthouses are often built with sustainable materials and energy-efficient systems. Many offer amenities like organic bedding, zero-waste toiletries, and locally sourced breakfasts. Staying in an eco-friendly guesthouse not only reduces your carbon footprint but also supports local businesses with sustainable practices.

8. Themed Apartments in the Medieval Village

In the outskirts of Nuremberg, a handful of themed apartments transport guests to different eras or fantasy worlds. Some are decorated to resemble medieval inns, complete with antique-style furniture and stone walls, while others play on themes like the Renaissance or fairytale settings. These apartments are family-friendly and often located in scenic countryside areas. Perfect for a memorable and immersive stay, they're a great choice if you're traveling with children or simply want a unique experience that's different from the usual hotel room.

9. Urban Garden Apartments

For travelers who enjoy a mix of urban convenience and nature, urban garden apartments provide a unique oasis in the city. These apartments are often situated in buildings with private gardens or terraces, filled with greenery, plants, and sometimes even small fountains. Staying in an urban garden apartment is ideal for unwinding after a day of exploring, as you can enjoy the fresh air and a bit of greenery without leaving the city.

10. Boutique Guesthouses in Craft Districts

Nuremberg's craft districts, known for their artisan shops and workshops, are home to boutique guesthouses with one-of-a-kind decor and locally inspired furnishings. These guesthouses celebrate the region's artistic traditions, with rooms often decorated by local artists, handmade furniture, and walls adorned with crafts from nearby studios. Staying in one of these boutique guesthouses allows you to fully immerse yourself in Nuremberg's cultural landscape and is ideal for art enthusiasts and anyone interested in supporting local artisans.

4.0 TOP ATTRACTIONS

4.1 NUREMBERG CASTLE

Nuremberg Castle is a cornerstone of the city's medieval charm and historical significance. Standing proudly on a sandstone ridge overlooking the old town, this mighty fortress complex is one of the most important medieval fortifications in Europe. Built around the 11th century and continually expanded over centuries, it reflects Nuremberg's rise as an imperial city and provides visitors a fascinating glimpse into its rich past.

A Walk Through History

Nuremberg Castle is not just one structure; it's a complex of fortifications that includes the **Kaiserburg** (Imperial Castle), **Burgrave's Castle**, and **Free Imperial City buildings**. Each section of the castle tells a story of different powers that ruled and shaped Nuremberg. The Kaiserburg was a favored residence for German kings and emperors in the Holy Roman Empire, while the Burgrave's Castle represented the city's noble families. Together, these fortified buildings made Nuremberg an imperial stronghold and a significant political center.

During World War II, Nuremberg Castle sustained severe damage from bombings, but a dedicated reconstruction effort restored its former glory. Today, the castle stands as a powerful reminder of resilience and the cultural spirit of the city.

Key Attractions and Highlights

When visiting Nuremberg Castle, you'll encounter a mix of breathtaking views, architectural marvels, and insightful exhibitions. Here are some highlights not to miss:

The Sinwell Tower:

Climb this historic watchtower for a panoramic view of Nuremberg's old town and surrounding areas. Originally built in the 13th century, the Sinwell Tower offers sweeping views that are perfect for photography or simply taking in the beauty of the city.

The Deep Well:

This medieval marvel is 47 meters deep and was essential for the castle's water supply. A guided demonstration provides insight into the construction and operation of this fascinating feature and highlights the castle's self-sufficiency.

Imperial Castle Museum:

Housed within the Kaiserburg, this museum immerses visitors in the life of the medieval elite, featuring historical artifacts like weapons, armor, and relics of the Holy Roman Empire. The exhibits offer a compelling perspective on Nuremberg's role as an imperial power center.

The Double Chapel:

One of the architectural gems of the Kaiserburg, this two-story Romanesque chapel dates back to the 11th century. Its unique structure, featuring one chapel built directly above another, was used by royalty and nobility, showcasing the wealth and artistry of medieval craftsmanship.

Visitor Experience and Practical Tips

Nuremberg Castle is open to visitors year-round, though hours may vary seasonally. A tour of the castle typically takes around two hours, allowing ample time to explore and admire the details. To enhance your visit, consider an audio or guided tour, as these provide deep insights into the historical context of each section and reveal fascinating stories about the people who once lived here.

The castle grounds are partially free to explore, while some areas, like the museum and Sinwell

Tower, require an entry fee. Discounts are often available for families, seniors, and students.

Best Time to Visit:

For the most comfortable experience, visit Nuremberg Castle in the spring or early fall when the weather is mild, and the crowds are smaller. Winter offers a unique ambiance, especially around Christmas, when the city transforms with festive decorations and Nuremberg's renowned Christmas Market nearby.

4.2 THE DOCUMENTATION CENTER NAZI PARTY RALLY GROUNDS

The Documentation Center Nazi Party Rally Grounds in Nuremberg is one of Germany's most profound and reflective historical sites. Situated on the former grounds where the Nazi Party held its massive rallies in the 1930s, this center is both a museum and educational institution, providing critical insights into Nazi ideology, propaganda, and the devastating impact of World War II. This is a must-visit for anyone seeking to understand the historical roots of Nazi power, the horrors of its regime, and Germany's post-war journey towards remembrance and accountability.

History and Context

The Nazi Party Rally Grounds were developed between 1933 and 1938, encompassing an area of about 11 square kilometers (4.25 square miles). Adolf Hitler personally selected Nuremberg due to its central location in Germany and its symbolic connection to the Holy Roman Empire. The grounds hosted rallies designed to inspire loyalty, foster propaganda, and promote Nazi ideology on an unprecedented scale. Architect Albert Speer, commissioned by Hitler, designed grandiose structures, including the Zeppelin Field and the Congress Hall, intended to project the regime's power and control. However, many of these projects were never completed, as World War II derailed further construction.

In the aftermath of the war, the rally grounds were left as stark reminders of this dark era. In the 1980s and 1990s, local and national authorities began discussions on how to handle the site, eventually deciding to create the Documentation Center in the Congress Hall. Opened in 2001, the Documentation Center presents the story of Nazi terror with the goal of educating future generations about the dangers of totalitarianism.

The Exhibition: "Fascination and Terror"

The permanent exhibition, titled **"Fascination and Terror"**, is housed in the northern wing of the Congress Hall. It guides visitors through the origins, rise, and destructive impact of the Nazi regime, focusing on how the National Socialists manipulated the German populace and consolidated power. Key topics include the political and social context of the 1920s, Hitler's ascent, and the establishment of a dictatorial state. The exhibition utilizes multimedia presentations, photographs, and eyewitness accounts, making the experience immersive and deeply moving.

Visitors follow a chronological path through a series of rooms that cover various aspects of Nazi history, including propaganda, antisemitism, the persecution of minorities, and the Holocaust. The exhibits critically examine how these rally grounds were utilized to glorify the Nazi regime, foster nationalistic fervor, and propagate messages of hate and division. The exhibition closes with sections on Germany's denazification efforts and the Nuremberg Trials, marking the beginning of justice and accountability after the war.

Architecture and Design

Albert Speer's original design for the Congress Hall was inspired by the Colosseum in Rome, intended to be a testament to the Nazi regime's permanence and power. Standing unfinished today, the Congress Hall is a chilling relic of Nazi ambitions. Its sheer size, massive pillars, and austere architecture still convey a sense of intimidation, helping visitors understand the scale of Nazi propaganda efforts. In a powerful juxtaposition, a modern glass and steel walkway now cuts diagonally through the structure, symbolizing transparency and the post-war democratic principles that challenge the oppressive history of this site.

The Documentation Center's modern design also reflects Germany's efforts to confront its past with openness and humility. Architect Günther Domenig designed the current exhibition space, adding elements that contrast with the original building's design to create a space where education replaces propaganda.

Exploring the Grounds

The rally grounds themselves include several significant sites beyond the Documentation Center. The Zeppelin Field, where Hitler delivered his speeches to vast crowds, still exists and offers a haunting glimpse into the scale of these gatherings. While the grandstands have largely deteriorated, a few structures remain, and interpretive panels help visitors imagine the rallies that once took place there. The Great Road, a massive stone-paved axis intended for military parades, stretches over a kilometer and serves as another reminder of the militaristic nature of Nazi Germany.

Visitor Information

Location: Bayernstrasse 110, Nuremberg, Germany

Hours: The Documentation Center is open daily, with limited hours on holidays. It's recommended to check the website for specific timings as they may vary.

Entry Fees: Tickets can be purchased on-site or online, with discounted rates available for students and families. Guided tours, available in English and German, offer additional insights and context for a deeper understanding of the exhibits.

Visitor Tips:

- **Time Required:** Allow at least 2–3 hours to explore the center thoroughly, especially if you want to take in the full exhibition and explore the rally grounds.

- **Audio Guides**: Available in multiple languages, audio guides are highly recommended for a comprehensive experience.

- **Guided Tours**: Consider joining a guided tour for added insights into the history and architecture.

- **Reflective Space**: The nature of the exhibits can be emotionally heavy. Take time to process and reflect, especially in designated quiet areas within the museum.

Why Visit?

The Documentation Center Nazi Party Rally Grounds is not only a place of historical significance but also a vital educational experience that confronts the atrocities of Nazi

Germany head-on. Its mission is to ensure that the lessons of the past are not forgotten and that the horrors of dictatorship, hate, and intolerance are never repeated. Visiting the Documentation Center is a deeply meaningful way to engage with history, understand the complexities of Germany's past, and reflect on the importance of vigilance and education in preserving democracy.

4.3 ALBRECHT DÜRER'S HOUSE

Albrecht Dürer's House is one of Nuremberg's most treasured landmarks, offering an intimate look into the life and legacy of Germany's most renowned Renaissance artist. Located near Nuremberg Castle in the picturesque old town, this historic half-timbered building was both Dürer's residence and workshop from 1509 until his death in 1528. Today, the house stands as a museum dedicated to his life and art, providing visitors with a fascinating experience that bridges five centuries.

Historical Background

Built in 1420, Albrecht Dürer's House is one of the few homes from this era to have survived the destruction of World War II. Dürer, celebrated for his masterful engravings, paintings, and prints, lived and worked here during the height of his career. The house represents not only his artistic achievements but also the lifestyle of Nuremberg's affluent class during the late Middle Ages. Restored and maintained with care, it now welcomes visitors from around the

146

world to step back into a time when Nuremberg was a hub of art, culture, and commerce.

Inside the Museum

The museum is thoughtfully curated across four floors, each offering insight into different facets of Dürer's life and work. Visitors can explore:

1. **The Studio and Printing Room**:

On the first floor, you'll find the artist's studio, where he worked on his woodcuts and engravings. Skilled guides demonstrate the printing techniques Dürer used, allowing visitors to see how he transformed drawings into detailed prints. This hands-on experience is especially popular, giving a rare look into Renaissance printmaking.

2. **Period Rooms**:

Throughout the house, several rooms are preserved to reflect the domestic setting of Dürer's time. Original furnishings and period-appropriate decor help recreate the ambiance of the early 16th century. Visitors can see Dürer's dining room, kitchen, and his workshop—spaces that offer a glimpse of his daily life.

3. **Exhibits of Dürer's Works**:

Although the house doesn't hold originals of Dürer's most famous works, it does showcase high-quality reproductions and facsimiles. From "Praying Hands" to "Melancholia I," these reproductions highlight the range of his artistry. The exhibition also includes copies of Dürer's self-portraits, such as his famous "Self-Portrait at Twenty-Eight," allowing visitors to appreciate his skill and attention to detail.

4. **Interactive and Multimedia Displays**:

The museum is well-suited for modern visitors with engaging multimedia exhibits that provide context for Dürer's life and artistic development. Informative displays shed light on Nuremberg's role as a cultural center, Dürer's friendships with intellectuals, and his influence on future generations of artists.

5. **Guided Tours and Insights from "Agnes Dürer"**: One of the unique features of the museum is its guided tours led by a costumed interpreter playing Agnes, Dürer's wife. Through her character,

visitors receive an immersive narrative about Dürer's life, personality, and work. These tours bring a personal touch to the visit and are highly recommended for a deeper, more interactive experience.

Events and Educational Programs

Albrecht Dürer's House also hosts a range of events throughout the year, including workshops, lectures, and special exhibits that delve into various aspects of Dürer's techniques and artistic influence. Art enthusiasts and families alike will find these activities enriching, as they offer practical insights into Dürer's work and the Renaissance era. The museum's workshops are especially popular with young visitors, fostering a deeper appreciation for art and history.

Practical Information

- **Location:**

The house is situated at Albrecht-Dürer-Straße 39, within easy walking distance from Nuremberg Castle and other key landmarks.

- **Opening Hours**: The museum is generally open daily, though hours may vary, especially on holidays. Checking the official website before your visit is recommended.

- **Tickets**: Admission fees are modest, with discounts available for students and families. Guided tours with the "Agnes Dürer" character may require an additional fee.

- **Accessibility**: While some parts of the house are accessible, the upper floors may be challenging for those with mobility issues due to the building's historical structure.

Why Visit Albrecht Dürer's House?

Albrecht Dürer's House is more than a museum—it's an authentic journey into the past. Whether you're an art lover, history buff, or curious traveler, this museum offers a unique opportunity to connect with Nuremberg's rich cultural heritage and understand the legacy of one of Germany's most celebrated artists. A visit to this house is a perfect addition to any Nuremberg itinerary, making it easy to appreciate the genius of Albrecht Dürer and the vibrant world of Renaissance Europe.

4.4 THE OLD TOWN (ALTSTADT)

Nuremberg's Old Town (Altstadt) is a beautiful fusion of medieval charm, historic landmarks, and vibrant culture that takes visitors back through centuries of history. Nestled within the city walls, the Altstadt is divided by the Pegnitz River, creating two distinct parts: St. Lorenz (southern part) and St. Sebald (northern part), named after their respective medieval churches. This iconic district is a must-visit for first-time travelers and returning visitors alike, offering a

captivating   journey   through   architectural
marvels, cozy squares, and lively markets.

1. Historic Landmarks and Architecture

One of the most striking features of Nuremberg's
Altstadt   is   its   well-preserved   medieval
architecture. The imposing Nuremberg Castle
(Kaiserburg), a series of fortified buildings
dating back to the 11th century, towers over the
city. Visitors can explore the castle's interiors,
including the imperial rooms, deep well, and

Sinwell Tower, which offers breathtaking panoramic views of Nuremberg's rooftops.

The medieval character of the Old Town is further emphasized by its city walls, which encircle much of the Altstadt. Originally constructed for defense, these walls date back to the 14th century and stretch for over 5 kilometers, punctuated by imposing towers and gates. The walls stand as a testament to Nuremberg's historical importance and resilience, having been largely restored after WWII.

2. Churches and Religious Sites

The Old Town's skyline is dominated by two magnificent Gothic churches: St. Lorenz Church (Lorenzkirche) and St. Sebaldus Church (Sebalduskirche). St. Lorenz, with its towering twin spires, is renowned for its intricate Gothic architecture and stunning rose window. The interior houses beautiful stained-glass windows, sculptures, and artworks that transport visitors back to the 15th century.

St. Sebaldus Church, named after Nuremberg's patron saint, is one of the oldest churches in the city, dating back to the 13th century. It contains impressive medieval art, including an exquisite bronze tomb of Saint Sebaldus, crafted by the sculptor Peter Vischer the Elder. Both churches are must-visit sites, offering insight into Nuremberg's religious heritage.

3. Market Squares and Shopping Streets

The Hauptmarkt (Main Market Square) is the heart of the Altstadt and comes alive throughout the year with colorful stalls selling local produce, flowers, crafts, and souvenirs. This square is particularly enchanting during December, when it transforms into the famous

Christkindlesmarkt (Christmas Market). Visitors flock to this market for festive treats, mulled wine, and beautifully crafted holiday decorations.

In the Hauptmarkt, visitors will also find the iconic Schöner Brunnen (Beautiful Fountain). Adorned with intricate statues, this 14th-century fountain is a striking symbol of Nuremberg, and local legend suggests that turning the golden ring embedded in its iron gate brings good luck.

For those who enjoy shopping, Karolinenstraße and Breite Gasse are two popular pedestrian streets filled with shops, boutiques, and cafes. From traditional handicrafts to modern retail brands, these streets offer a mix of local and international shopping experiences.

4. Museums and Cultural Spots

The Old Town is rich with museums that cater to diverse interests. Albrecht Dürer's House, where the famous German Renaissance artist lived and worked, offers a fascinating glimpse into the life and art of Dürer. Visitors can explore rooms filled with period furniture, a printmaking studio, and art displays, guided by insightful commentary on Dürer's life.

For history enthusiasts, the City Museum Fembohaus provides an immersive experience in Nuremberg's history, housed in a beautifully preserved Renaissance merchant's house.

Additionally, the Toy Museum (Spielzeugmuseum) is a delightful spot, especially for families, as it showcases a charming collection of toys from different eras, reflecting Nuremberg's long-standing reputation as a center of toy manufacturing.

5. Dining and Local Flavors

Exploring the Altstadt is bound to work up an appetite, and the Old Town's culinary offerings don't disappoint. Local eateries, beer halls, and restaurants serve up traditional Franconian dishes, like the famous Nürnberger Bratwurst—small, flavorful sausages often served with sauerkraut and pretzels. Be sure to also try Lebkuchen (gingerbread), a Nuremberg specialty that originated here and can be found at bakeries and markets throughout the Old Town.

Many establishments around the Hauptmarkt and the riverside offer cozy atmospheres and outdoor seating, allowing diners to soak in the views of medieval buildings and cobbled streets. Whether you're in the mood for hearty local fare or a quaint café experience, the Altstadt's dining scene offers a range of options.

6. Events and Festivities

Throughout the year, Nuremberg's Altstadt hosts various events and festivals that add to its vibrant character. Apart from the Christmas Market, the Old Town Festival (Altstadtfest) in September celebrates local culture with folk music, performances, and traditional Franconian food and drink. It's a festive opportunity to experience Nuremberg's culture among locals and visitors alike.

7. Exploring by Foot

One of the best ways to experience the Altstadt is by walking through its narrow cobblestone streets, hidden alleys, and picturesque squares. The Old Town's compact layout allows visitors to stroll between landmarks, shops, and restaurants with ease. Guided walking tours are available and offer insightful stories about Nuremberg's history, architecture, and culture. For a self-guided experience, plenty of signposts and information boards help guide visitors through the main sights and historical points of interest.

4.5 NUREMBERG ZOO

Nestled within the lush grounds of the historic Reichswald Forest, Nuremberg Zoo (Tiergarten Nürnberg) is one of Germany's oldest and most celebrated zoological gardens. Founded in 1912, it spans over 170 acres, offering an idyllic natural setting where visitors can explore animal habitats that blend harmoniously into the landscape, creating a unique and immersive experience for both first-time and returning visitors.

A Unique Setting Among European Zoos

One of the aspects that sets Nuremberg Zoo apart is its emphasis on recreating authentic habitats for its animals. Instead of a traditional zoo with cages and enclosures, Nuremberg Zoo incorporates the surrounding forest's natural features, such as ponds, creeks, and rolling hills, making it feel more like a wildlife sanctuary. This design creates an environment that closely mirrors each animal's native habitat, enhancing both the animals' welfare and visitors' viewing experience.

Animal Attractions and Conservation Efforts

Home to over 300 species and approximately 3,000 animals, Nuremberg Zoo is known for its diverse wildlife, ranging from majestic big cats and playful primates to fascinating marine life. Highlights include the dolphin lagoon and the manatee house. Nuremberg Zoo is one of the few zoos in Europe to house manatees, and the only one in Germany to offer a dolphin lagoon, where guests can watch dolphins swim and perform acrobatic tricks in an open-air pool.

The zoo is also a leader in animal conservation, both locally and globally. They collaborate with wildlife conservation projects worldwide, especially focusing on breeding endangered species. Through careful management and partnerships with international zoos, Nuremberg Zoo actively contributes to the conservation of rare animals like snow leopards, Siberian tigers, and endangered bird species.

The Dolphin Lagoon and Manatee House

A particularly popular area, the dolphin lagoon draws visitors from all over. This open-air facility lets guests view dolphins up close in a more naturalistic environment. Connected to this is the manatee house, where the gentle and rare manatees glide through water in a serene setting. These attractions not only entertain but also educate visitors on marine conservation, emphasizing the importance of protecting our oceans and aquatic animals.

Kids' Paradise: A Family-Friendly Zoo

Families visiting Nuremberg Zoo will find a range of kid-friendly activities designed to keep young minds engaged. The petting zoo allows children to interact with domestic animals like goats, sheep, and donkeys, fostering a sense of curiosity and care for animals. There's also an adventure playground, complete with slides, swings, and a climbing wall, providing children with a fun place to let off some steam during their visit.

Nuremberg Zoo also hosts interactive workshops and educational programs for children and teens, making it an enriching experience for all ages. Many visitors find that a trip to Nuremberg Zoo is an excellent opportunity for children to learn about animal care, ecosystems, and conservation efforts.

Practical Information for Visitors

Nuremberg Zoo is open year-round, although hours may vary depending on the season. It's easily accessible by public transportation, with a tram line that stops directly in front of the entrance. For those driving, there is ample parking available. Tickets can be purchased on-site or online, with options for family passes and seasonal passes.

The zoo offers several dining options, including on-site restaurants and snack stands that serve a mix of traditional Bavarian dishes and family-friendly fare. There are also picnic areas for those who prefer to bring their own food, allowing visitors to spend the entire day without having to leave the grounds.

Tips for Making the Most of Your Visit

- **Arrive Early**: Nuremberg Zoo is extensive, so arriving early gives you plenty of time to explore at a leisurely pace and attend animal feedings or demonstrations.

- **Bring Comfortable Shoes**: The zoo's large, naturalistic layout involves plenty of walking, often over uneven terrain.

- **Check the Feeding Schedule**: Nuremberg Zoo organizes scheduled feedings and keeper talks for certain animals, including the lions and dolphins. These events offer unique insights into the animals' lives and behaviors.

- **Don't Miss the Dolphin Show**:

The dolphin shows are a highlight and tend to be popular, so be sure to check showtimes upon arrival.

Why Visit Nuremberg Zoo?

For animal lovers and families alike, Nuremberg Zoo provides a memorable experience that combines education, conservation, and a close connection to nature. Its focus on animal welfare and conservation, set within a peaceful forest landscape, makes it one of the most unique zoos in Europe. Whether you're looking to learn about exotic animals, entertain young children, or simply enjoy a day immersed in nature, a visit to Nuremberg Zoo is a perfect addition to your Nuremberg travel itinerary.

4.6 THE GERMAN NATIONAL MUSEUM

The German National Museum in Nuremberg, known as the Germanisches Nationalmuseum (GNM), is one of the most prominent and expansive museums dedicated to German art, culture, and history. Founded in 1852, it is located in the historic heart of Nuremberg and is a must-visit for anyone wanting to explore Germany's cultural heritage.

Historical Significance and Overview

The German National Museum has a deep historical connection to German identity. Originally founded to preserve and showcase artifacts of German-speaking regions, it has grown over the centuries into one of the largest cultural museums in the country, housing over 1.3 million objects. The museum's mission is to capture the essence of German culture across the centuries, and it does so with carefully curated exhibits and vast collections that range from the prehistoric to the modern era.

Architectural Marvel

The museum complex itself is architecturally significant, blending historic and modern elements. The entrance area, a striking glass-and-steel addition completed in the 1990s, connects seamlessly with older, preserved sections of the building, creating a dynamic interplay between past and present. The monastic cloister, medieval chapel, and historic city walls integrate into the museum's design, offering visitors a journey through time before even entering the galleries.

Collections and Exhibits

The German National Museum is organized thematically and spans a vast array of topics and time periods. The exhibits offer something for everyone, from lovers of fine art to those interested in science and technology, medieval artifacts, or modern cultural developments.

1. Prehistoric and Ancient Artifacts

The museum houses an impressive collection of artifacts from prehistoric and ancient times, including tools, pottery, and ceremonial items. These exhibits reveal much about the early lives of people in the German-speaking regions, showcasing the transition from nomadic societies to agricultural settlements.

2. Medieval and Renaissance Art

The German National Museum is especially known for its medieval and Renaissance collections, including notable works by Albrecht Dürer, Nuremberg's famous artist. Here, you can find paintings, sculptures, tapestries, and metalwork that reflect the height of German craftsmanship in the Middle Ages. Some masterpieces include religious artifacts, altarpieces, and intricately carved sculptures.

3. Applied Arts and Decorative Items

A section dedicated to decorative arts features items like furniture, porcelain, glassware, and textiles from various historical periods. This area gives a glimpse into domestic life, design evolution, and the tastes and trends of German society across the centuries.

4. Scientific Instruments and Technology

This collection highlights Germany's contributions to science and engineering, with displays of historic clocks, compasses, globes, and astronomical instruments. These artifacts underscore the region's influence in the fields of navigation, astronomy, and timekeeping.

5. Modern Art and Popular Culture

The museum also celebrates modern artistic and cultural movements, including contemporary art, posters, and film memorabilia. These exhibits reflect Germany's dynamic 20th-century history and evolving cultural landscape, providing insight into societal changes post-World War II.

6. Special Exhibitions

Throughout the year, the museum hosts special exhibitions that explore specific themes or focus on particular artists, periods, or styles. These temporary exhibits often incorporate multimedia presentations and interactive displays, adding a unique dimension to the museum experience.

Interactive and Educational Opportunities

The German National Museum offers various interactive experiences, making it an ideal destination for families and young travelers. Educational workshops, guided tours, and audio guides (available in multiple languages) allow visitors to delve deeper into specific topics. For children, the museum provides fun and engaging activities designed to introduce them to German history and culture.

The Museum Courtyard and Café

After exploring the galleries, visitors can relax in the museum's tranquil courtyard or visit the on-site café, which offers traditional German treats and light refreshments. The peaceful courtyard is a perfect spot to take a break, reflect, and enjoy the museum's unique architecture.

Visitor Information

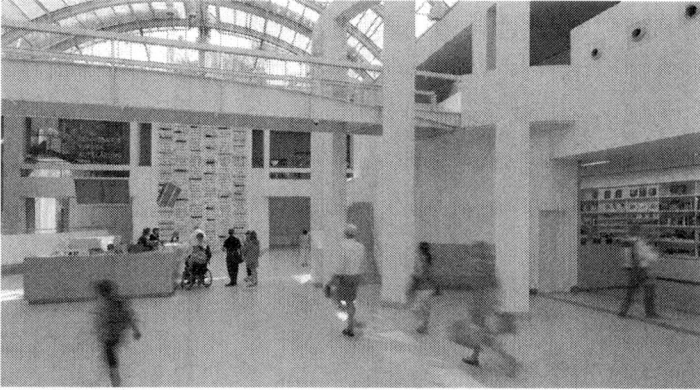

The German National Museum is easily accessible by public transportation and located near other notable sites, making it a convenient stop on a day of sightseeing. It's advisable to allocate at least half a day to fully explore the museum due to its size and extensive collections.

Tips for Visiting:

- Consider taking a guided tour to gain more insight into key pieces and exhibits.

- Check the museum's website in advance for information on temporary exhibitions and events.

- Allocate enough time to explore the museum's highlights without feeling rushed.

5.0 CULTURAL EXPERIENCES

5.1 NUREMBERG'S FESTIVALS AND EVENTS

Nuremberg is a city deeply rooted in tradition, yet it embraces modernity with a spirited blend of events that honor its past while celebrating the contemporary. With annual festivals ranging from world-famous holiday markets to historical reenactments, Nuremberg promises unforgettable experiences throughout the year.

1. Nuremberg Christkindlesmarkt

- **When**: Late November to December 24

- **Where**: Hauptmarkt (Main Market Square)

- **Why You Should Go**: Known as one of Germany's most iconic Christmas markets, the Christkindlesmarkt draws visitors worldwide with its charming wooden stalls, festive lights, and holiday cheer. The market's centerpiece is the "Christkind," a golden-robed angel who opens the festivities with a heartwarming prologue. Expect to find beautifully crafted gifts, aromatic gingerbread (Lebkuchen), and the cozy scent of mulled wine (Glühwein) in the air.

2. Nuremberg Old Town Festival (Altstadtfest)

- **When**: Mid-September

- **Where**: Nuremberg Old Town

- **Why You Should Go**: This festival is an immersive dive into Franconian culture, with traditional music, dance, and Franconian delicacies like sausages and beer filling the city. Over two weeks, locals and visitors alike celebrate with outdoor concerts, parades, and food stalls offering regional cuisine. A unique highlight is the "Fischerstechen" (Fishermen's Jousting), where competitors in small boats joust in the Pegnitz River—a must-see tradition.

3. Rock im Park Festival

- **When**: June

- **Where**: Zeppelinfeld, Dutzendteich Park

- **Why You Should Go**: As one of Germany's largest rock music festivals, Rock im Park brings together global and local rock, indie, and alternative music artists for a three-day celebration of music. This event draws an energetic crowd, transforming Nuremberg into a lively hub of music lovers. With several stages, a variety of food vendors, and camping options, Rock im Park promises an unforgettable, adrenaline-fueled experience.

4. Nürnberger Bardentreffen (Nuremberg Bard Meeting)

- **When**: Last weekend in July

- **Where**: Various locations in the Old Town

- **Why You Should Go**: Europe's largest free world music festival, Bardentreffen offers a vibrant mix of international music genres, from folk to jazz, blues to contemporary. Streets, squares, and hidden corners of the city come alive with artists performing for visitors of all ages. This family-friendly event, drawing musicians from all over the globe, allows you to wander through Nuremberg's historic streets while enjoying diverse sounds and cultures.

5. Blue Night (Blaue Nacht)

- **When**: May

- **Where**: Nuremberg Old Town

- **Why You Should Go**: This annual event turns Nuremberg into a magical canvas of art and light installations, with buildings bathed in blue hues. Local museums, galleries, and cultural institutions stay open late, offering special exhibitions and performances. Street artists, musicians, and performers fill the streets, creating an immersive cultural experience. The Blue

Night is an excellent way to explore Nuremberg's rich artistic scene in a surreal, dream-like atmosphere.

6. International Nuremberg Film Festival (Internationale Filmtage Nürnberg)

- **When**: Varies (typically fall)

- **Where**: Various cinemas and cultural venues

- **Why You Should Go**: Highlighting independent films and international cinema, this festival offers screenings, panel discussions, and workshops that attract filmmakers and enthusiasts from around the world. It's an ideal event for film lovers who appreciate thought-provoking and boundary-pushing cinema, providing an opportunity to see unique films that often don't reach mainstream theaters.

7. Volksfest (Nuremberg Folk Festival)

- **When**: Twice a year (Spring and Fall)

- **Where**: Dutzendteich Park

- **Why You Should Go**: This traditional folk festival is Nuremberg's answer to Oktoberfest. Expect lively music, thrilling carnival rides, and bustling beer tents serving local brews. Families, friends, and visitors come together to enjoy amusement rides, games, and Franconian delicacies. The Volksfest's family-friendly atmosphere, combined with its celebratory energy, makes it perfect for both locals and tourists.

5.2 MUSEUMS AND GALLERIES

Nuremberg's rich history and vibrant arts scene are displayed throughout its many museums and galleries, offering a journey from medieval times to modern-day masterpieces. Here's an overview of some must-visit spots for a well-rounded cultural experience.

Germanisches Nationalmuseum

The Germanisches Nationalmuseum is the largest museum of cultural history in the German-speaking world. Housing over 1.3 million objects, this museum provides a comprehensive view of German art, culture, and history from prehistoric times to the present. Visitors will find medieval weapons, Renaissance sculptures, Baroque paintings, and modern art exhibits. Highlights include the oldest surviving globe, Albrecht Dürer's sketches, and an expansive collection of folk art. With regular temporary exhibitions and a beautiful courtyard garden, the museum is a must-see for history and art enthusiasts alike.

Address: Kartäusergasse 1
Admission: Regular admission fees apply, with discounts for students and groups.

Albrecht Dürer's House

One of Nuremberg's most celebrated figures, Albrecht Dürer, lived and worked in this charming half-timbered house near the Imperial Castle. Albrecht Dürer's House is a well-preserved medieval home dedicated to his life and art. The museum displays reproductions of Dürer's famous works, original prints, and engravings, as well as interactive exhibits on his techniques. A unique feature is the "living history" tours, where actors in period costumes bring Dürer's life to the present. It's an intimate experience that lets visitors walk in the footsteps of Germany's Renaissance master.

Address: Albrecht-Dürer-Strasse 39

Admission: Reduced rates for families and groups; free entry on specific days.

Neues Museum – State Museum for Art and Design

For lovers of contemporary art, the Neues Museum is a bright, airy building that bridges the old town with Nuremberg's modern side. Known for its stunning architecture, the museum showcases a dynamic range of 20th and 21st-century art and design. Expect to see works by contemporary German artists alongside international names. The museum also holds rotating exhibitions that explore topics like photography, graphic design, and modern installation art, making every visit a fresh experience. Its minimalist design and light-filled spaces create an inspiring atmosphere for art enthusiasts.

Address: Klarissenplatz
Admission: Varies; discounts available for students and seniors.

Documentation Center Nazi Party Rally Grounds

Located on the former grounds of Nazi rallies, the Documentation Center offers a solemn exploration of the rise of the Nazi party and the consequences of World War II. The museum's permanent exhibition, "Fascination and Terror," delves into the propaganda, ideology, and architecture of the Nazi regime through photographs, films, and personal testimonies. The exhibit is designed to be informative yet reflective, encouraging visitors to confront and learn from the past. Audio guides are available, providing in-depth narratives about each exhibit.

Address: Bayernstraße 110
Admission: Fees apply; reduced rates for youth and students.

Toy Museum (Spielzeugmuseum)

Nuremberg has a long history as a center of toy-making, and the Toy Museum celebrates this legacy with a charming collection of toys from the 18th century to the present day. Visitors can explore rooms filled with antique dolls, model trains, tin soldiers, and even early electronic games. The interactive exhibits and dedicated play areas make it ideal for families, though it's just as fascinating for adults interested in the evolution of toys and children's culture over the centuries. The museum's collection offers a nostalgic journey that connects generations.

Address: Karlstraße 13-15
Admission: Affordable entry, with family and group rates.

Kunsthalle Nürnberg

The Kunsthalle Nürnberg is an esteemed gallery in Nuremberg's art scene, hosting changing exhibitions of contemporary works by international and German artists. Located in the historical city center, the gallery emphasizes experimental and innovative art forms, showcasing everything from sculpture to video installations. Each exhibit often delves into timely social issues, offering thought-provoking pieces and encouraging dialogue between artists and visitors. Art lovers interested in the cutting edge of the contemporary scene will appreciate this dynamic venue.

Address: Lorenzer Straße 32

Admission: Admission varies by exhibition.

Museum Tucherschloss and Hirsvogelsaal

For a taste of Renaissance aristocratic life, Museum Tucherschloss provides a peek into the lives of the Tucher family, one of Nuremberg's most influential noble families. The museum is set within the elegant Tucher mansion and features ornate period rooms, art, and valuable artifacts that reflect the city's golden age in the 16th century. The adjacent Hirsvogelsaal, an opulent hall with an intricately carved wooden ceiling and period decorations, often hosts events and concerts, offering a regal setting that transports visitors back in time.

Address: Hirschelgasse 9-11
Admission: Standard fees apply; combination tickets available.

Memorium Nuremberg Trials

This museum is a deeply moving tribute to one of the most significant events in modern history: the Nuremberg Trials. The Memorium Nuremberg Trials is located within the Palace of Justice, where prominent Nazi officials were prosecuted for crimes against humanity. The exhibition provides insight into the historical and legal significance of the trials, detailing how the international tribunal set a precedent for future human rights cases. Guided tours and video presentations offer a powerful exploration of justice and accountability.

Address: Bärenschanzstraße 72

Admission: Entry fees apply; guided tours recommended.

Tips for Museum-Goers

Plan Ahead: Many museums offer free or discounted entry on specific days, and some have extended evening hours.

Audio Guides:

Several museums, such as the Documentation Center, offer audio guides in multiple languages for a more immersive experience.

Combination Tickets: For those planning to visit multiple museums, combination tickets can often be purchased at a discount.

Seasonal Exhibitions
:

Keep an eye out for temporary exhibits, as Nuremberg's museums frequently rotate collections to keep the experience fresh for returning visitors.

These museums and galleries not only showcase Nuremberg's past but also demonstrate its commitment to preserving history while embracing contemporary art.

5.3 TRADITIONAL CRAFTS AND MARKETS

Nuremberg is renowned for its rich heritage of traditional crafts, which are celebrated in the city's vibrant markets. A visit to these markets not only offers an insight into the city's cultural history but also provides a unique shopping experience that combines local craftsmanship, historical ambiance, and lively festivities.

Nuremberg Crafts and Artisanship

For centuries, Nuremberg has been a hub for skilled artisans, from goldsmiths and potters to toy makers and woodcarvers. This long-standing tradition has shaped the city's reputation, especially in woodworking and metal crafts. Visitors will find various workshops and stores around Nuremberg where artisans continue to produce unique handmade items, maintaining skills that have been passed down through generations. Popular items include handcrafted jewelry, intricate wooden toys, beautifully designed pottery, and detailed leather goods, all of which are known for their durability and beauty.

Nuremberg's Toy-Making Tradition

One of the city's most famous crafts is toy making. Nuremberg earned the nickname "Toy City" (Spielzeugstadt) due to its historical role as a toy manufacturing center. This tradition dates back to the Middle Ages when wooden dolls, miniature figures, and marionettes made in Nuremberg became sought-after items across Europe. Today, visitors can explore this legacy at the Nuremberg Toy Museum, where antique toys and modern creations are on display, offering a nostalgic look into Nuremberg's playful history.

Handcrafted Gingerbread (Lebkuchen)

Nuremberg's gingerbread, known as Lebkuchen, is another iconic product. Dating back to the 14th century, Lebkuchen was first made by Franconian monks and has become a symbol of Nuremberg's culinary heritage. This delicately spiced gingerbread is crafted with a blend of nuts, honey, and exotic spices and often decorated with intricate designs. Lebkuchen is widely available throughout the year but becomes especially popular during the holiday season, with many bakeries and stalls offering fresh varieties that make for ideal souvenirs.

Exploring Nuremberg's Markets

Nuremberg's markets are where the city's craft traditions come to life, providing a unique setting to experience local culture. The lively atmosphere, paired with the stalls filled with handcrafted items and regional delicacies, makes these markets an essential part of any visit to Nuremberg.

Hauptmarkt (Main Market)

The Hauptmarkt in Nuremberg's Old Town is the city's largest and most famous market square. Held year-round, this bustling marketplace is filled with stalls selling everything from fresh produce and flowers to traditional crafts and handmade gifts. On weekdays, you'll find local farmers and artisans offering seasonal fruits, vegetables, cheeses, and honey. The Hauptmarkt's striking centerpiece, the "Beautiful Fountain" (Schöner Brunnen), adds to the charm, making it a memorable spot to explore.

Christkindlesmarkt (Christmas Market)

Arguably the most famous market in Nuremberg, the Christkindlesmarkt (Christ Child Market) is celebrated as one of Germany's oldest and most traditional Christmas markets. Dating back to the 16th century, the Christkindlesmarkt attracts visitors from around the world who come to experience its festive atmosphere and charming stalls. Held in the Hauptmarkt during Advent, this market is a wonderland of twinkling lights, aromatic mulled wine, and holiday treats. Stalls feature handmade ornaments, toys, and gingerbread—perfect for holiday shopping or simply soaking up the Christmas spirit.

Nuremberg's Christkindlesmarkt is also known for its "Rauschgoldengel," or "gold-foil angel," an emblem of Nuremberg's Christmas celebrations. These delicate golden angels, crafted by local artisans, have become a traditional decoration for Christmas trees and an iconic symbol of the city. They make for a meaningful keepsake, embodying the festive spirit of Nuremberg's holiday season.

Handwerkerhof (Craftsmen's Courtyard)

Located near the King's Gate in the Old Town, the Handwerkerhof (Craftsmen's Courtyard) is a charming, medieval-style market dedicated to preserving Nuremberg's artisanal crafts. Here, visitors can step back in time as they wander through narrow alleys lined with half-timbered houses that host small workshops and boutique stores. Craftsmen and women demonstrate traditional techniques, including glassblowing, leatherworking, and pottery-making. You'll also find locally made Franconian specialties and handicrafts, from jewelry to wood carvings. The Handwerkerhof is a great place to find unique souvenirs and experience the city's enduring artisanal culture.

Spring and Autumn Markets

Nuremberg's Spring Market (Ostermarkt) and Autumn Market (Herbstmarkt) offer seasonal shopping experiences filled with regional crafts and local flavors. The Spring Market, held before Easter, features hand-painted eggs, floral arrangements, and seasonal foods, while the Autumn Market, typically in September, showcases harvest products, such as honey, fresh cider, and artisan cheeses. These markets highlight Nuremberg's seasonal traditions and provide a perfect opportunity to enjoy the city's changing landscapes and culinary offerings.

Tips for Enjoying Nuremberg's Markets and Crafts

- **Timing Your Visit**: The Christmas Market can get very crowded, especially on weekends. Visiting on weekday mornings can make for a more relaxed experience.

- **Supporting Local Artisans**: Purchasing items directly from artisans at these markets not only supports local craftsmanship but also ensures you're getting an authentic piece of Nuremberg's heritage.

- **Sampling Local Treats**:

Don't miss the chance to try some of Nuremberg's traditional foods, especially the gingerbread and bratwurst. Many market stalls offer small portions or samples to try before you buy.

- **Capturing Memories**:

Nuremberg's markets are full of picturesque details, from the medieval-inspired Handwerkerhof to the festive decorations at the Christkindlesmarkt. Bring a camera to capture these moments.

5.4 LOCAL MUSIC AND THEATER

Nuremberg has a vibrant cultural scene, making it a rich destination for music and theater enthusiasts. The city offers a mix of classical and contemporary performances, housed in historic venues that amplify the artistic ambiance. Whether you're a fan of symphonies, operas, or modern theater, Nuremberg provides memorable experiences in all these realms.

Classical Music and Opera

Nuremberg's dedication to classical music is well-established, with the Staatstheater Nürnberg (Nuremberg State Theatre) at the forefront. This iconic venue, one of the largest in Germany, features an impressive repertoire of operas, ballets, and symphonic performances throughout the year. With its grand architecture and rich history, the Staatstheater is a must-visit for any classical music lover.

The Nuremberg Symphony Orchestra also deserves special mention. Known for their inspiring performances, they offer an extensive schedule of concerts, from grand symphonies to chamber music events. Concerts are often held in beautiful venues like the Meistersingerhalle, a modern concert hall with superb acoustics, named in honor of the "Meistersinger von Nürnberg," a famous opera by Richard Wagner. Here, locals and visitors alike gather to enjoy performances that range from classical masterpieces to innovative contemporary compositions.

Modern and Experimental Music

Beyond classical music, Nuremberg has a thriving scene for modern and experimental genres. The Künstlerhaus is an essential destination for alternative music and cultural events. Located in the old city, this unique cultural center offers a stage for everything from jazz and electronic music to avant-garde performances. It's a place where local artists and musicians experiment and engage the audience with new styles and genres, and it's also home to several annual music festivals.

Nuremberg also embraces the sounds of rock, pop, and indie music with various live venues around the city. Hirsch, a popular music venue, hosts performances by local bands, international artists, and everyone in between. The atmosphere here is vibrant, with an intimate feel that brings fans close to the artists, creating a memorable live music experience.

Annual Music Festivals

One of the highlights of Nuremberg's music calendar is the Rock im Park festival, held every June. Drawing music fans from across Europe, Rock im Park features a diverse lineup of rock, punk, and metal acts, making it one of the biggest music festivals in Germany. The energy and spirit of this festival capture the dynamic side of Nuremberg's music scene, showcasing both global superstars and emerging bands in a high-energy outdoor setting.

For jazz lovers, Bardentreffen is a beloved summer festival featuring performances by folk, jazz, and world music artists. Held across multiple open-air stages throughout the old town, Bardentreffen attracts musicians and music lovers from all over the world. This free festival is a wonderful way to experience Nuremberg's communal spirit as locals and visitors gather to enjoy the eclectic sounds filling the streets.

Theater and Performing Arts

Theater holds a prominent place in Nuremberg's cultural landscape. The Staatstheater Nürnberg not only excels in opera and ballet but also presents dramatic plays and musicals, with performances often inspired by both German and international literature. Productions range from Shakespearean classics to German masterpieces, as well as contemporary works exploring current social themes.

For those interested in more intimate and experimental theater, the Theater Pfütze provides a unique experience. This theater, especially known for its productions aimed at families and younger audiences, showcases inventive performances that blend storytelling with imaginative staging and interactive elements. It's a great option for families traveling with children who want a culturally enriching experience.

The Tafelhalle is another must-visit for theater lovers, offering a mix of modern theater, dance, and multimedia performances. Known for its contemporary approach, Tafelhalle is the place to experience cutting-edge German theater. It hosts everything from spoken word and improv to contemporary dance, making it a hub for the avant-garde performing arts.

Puppetry and Traditional Performances

Nuremberg has a fascinating tradition in puppetry, tracing back centuries and still present in local culture. The Figurentheater Salz+Pfeffer specializes in puppet theater, offering shows that appeal to both children and adults. This small theater provides an enchanting journey into the world of puppetry, combining traditional techniques with modern storytelling. It's a special experience, particularly for those interested in the unique blend of craftsmanship and performance that puppetry offers.

Local Tips

For those wanting a deeper dive into Nuremberg's performing arts, consider visiting the Kultur Information center for up-to-date listings of events, shows, and ticket information. This is especially helpful if you're looking for last-minute tickets or want recommendations based on your interests. Additionally, exploring lesser-known venues or attending local festivals is a great way to experience the city's artistic spirit beyond the well-known stages.

6.0 DINING AND NIGHTLIFE

6.1 TRADITIONAL NUREMBERG CUISINE

Nuremberg's cuisine is a blend of hearty Franconian tradition, medieval influences, and locally sourced ingredients, offering visitors a unique taste of German culinary heritage. For food lovers, the city is renowned for a few quintessential dishes and drinks that should not be missed.

1. Nuremberg Bratwurst

At the heart of Nuremberg's culinary reputation is its world-famous Nürnberger Rostbratwurst, a small, delicately seasoned sausage. These sausages are usually only about 7-9 centimeters long, but don't let their size fool you – they pack a flavorful punch! Traditionally, these sausages are grilled over a beechwood fire, which gives them a distinct smoky taste. Locals enjoy them served three-at-a-time on a fresh roll, known as "Drei im Weckla," or plated with sauerkraut or potato salad.

2. Lebkuchen (Gingerbread)

Nuremberg's gingerbread, or Lebkuchen, has been a holiday staple since the Middle Ages. Made with a blend of honey, nuts, and spices, this gingerbread is typically softer and richer than other varieties, often topped with a thin icing or covered in dark chocolate. During the holiday season, the entire city smells of gingerbread, thanks to the many bakeries producing it fresh. Be sure to try Elisenlebkuchen, a premium variation with a higher nut content and no flour, named after the patron saint of gingerbread bakers.

3. Schäufele (Pork Shoulder)

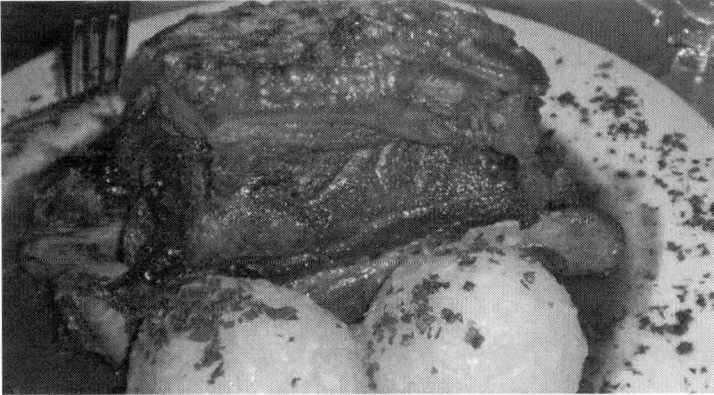

Schäufele is a hearty dish that showcases Nuremberg's love for pork. This roasted pork shoulder is slowly cooked with a crispy crust, seasoned with caraway, and served with a rich, flavorful gravy. It's typically accompanied by traditional potato dumplings, known as Klöße, and red cabbage, making it a perfect comfort meal for colder days. The dish's name comes from the shovel-like shape of the shoulder blade bone, and it's a must-try for fans of roasted meats.

4. Fränkischer Sauerbraten (Franconian Pot Roast)

Originating in Franconia, Sauerbraten is a pot roast marinated in vinegar, spices, and onions for several days to develop a unique tangy flavor. In Nuremberg, it's often served with a dark, sweet sauce enriched with gingerbread crumbs, which adds a delightful sweetness. Like Schäufele, it's commonly paired with potato dumplings and a side of red cabbage, embodying the region's signature balance of sweet and savory.

5. Blue Carp (Blaue Zipfel)

Fish lovers should try Blaue Zipfel, a Franconian specialty involving sausages poached in a broth of vinegar, onions, and spices. Traditionally served in a broth alongside onions and mustard, it's distinctively tangy and pairs excellently with a side of dark rye bread. While less common than bratwurst, it's a fascinating dish that highlights Nuremberg's versatility in sausage preparation.

6. Local Beers and Franconian Wine

Nuremberg's Franconian heritage extends into its drinking culture, making it a prime destination for lovers of traditional beer and wine. The city offers various Kellerbier (cellar beers), which are unfiltered and have a fresh, slightly cloudy appearance. For those preferring wine, the region's Franconian white wines, particularly Silvaner and Müller-Thurgau, offer crisp and refreshing notes that pair wonderfully with traditional dishes. Don't miss a visit to a local beer cellar or wine tavern for an authentic Franconian drinking experience.

7. Zwetschgenbaames (Cured Smoked Meat)

Another Franconian specialty, Zwetschgenbaames, is a cured and smoked pork shoulder that is sliced thin and served with dark bread, pickles, and mustard. Its name comes from the traditional smoking process, which often involves plum wood for an added layer of flavor. This dish is popular for a quick snack or a light meal and pairs wonderfully with a local beer.

8. Kirschenmännla (Cherry Men Cookies)

For dessert, Kirschenmännla is a traditional Nuremberg treat featuring shortbread cookies topped with cherries and nuts. These delicate, buttery cookies offer a taste of local traditions, often prepared around Christmas, but are enjoyed throughout the year. The sweetness of cherries balances the richness of the shortbread, creating a memorable bite-sized indulgence.

6.2 TOP RESTAURANTS TO TRY

Nuremberg is celebrated for its culinary scene, where traditional Franconian flavors meet modern gastronomy. Here are some must-try restaurants that offer authentic and unique dining experiences for every type of traveler.

1. Bratwursthäusle

One of Nuremberg's most iconic dining spots, Bratwursthäusle is famed for its traditional Nürnberger sausages. This historic restaurant, located near the Hauptmarkt, prepares its sausages over an open beechwood fire, giving them a smoky, rich flavor. Pair your sausages with sauerkraut and fresh horseradish for an authentic Franconian experience. The restaurant's rustic ambiance adds to the charm, making it a perfect stop for lunch or dinner after exploring the Old Town.

Location: Rathausplatz 1, 90403 Nuremberg

Must-try: Nürnberger Rostbratwurst with sauerkraut and horseradish

2. Essigbrätlein

For fine dining enthusiasts, Essigbrätlein is a Michelin-starred gem in the heart of Nuremberg. Known for its seasonal and creative dishes, this restaurant uses high-quality local ingredients to deliver exquisite meals that highlight Franconian flavors with a modern twist. The menu changes

frequently, so each visit offers a fresh culinary surprise. With only a few tables, it's recommended to make a reservation well in advance.

Location: Weinmarkt 3, 90403 Nuremberg

Must-try: Seasonal tasting menu (often featuring unique combinations like root vegetables with Franconian herbs)

3. Hausbrauerei Altstadthof

This charming brewery-restaurant is a top pick for beer lovers and those interested in hearty, regional cuisine. Hausbrauerei Altstadthof specializes in handcrafted beers and serves dishes that perfectly complement its brews. Try the Schäufele, a Franconian pork shoulder dish with a crispy crust, served with potato dumplings. The brewery also offers guided tours for those curious about Nuremberg's long beer-making traditions.

Location: Bergstraße 19, 90403 Nuremberg

Must-try: Schäufele with potato dumplings, paired with Altstadthof's red beer

4. Café Bar Katz

For a casual yet elegant dining experience, Café Bar Katz is ideal for brunch, lunch, or dinner. Known for its cozy, bohemian atmosphere and vibrant outdoor seating, it serves a mix of Mediterranean-inspired and Franconian dishes.

The menu offers a selection of fresh, seasonal ingredients and vegetarian options, catering to a variety of tastes. Whether you're enjoying a coffee in the morning or a glass of wine in the evening, Café Bar Katz is a great place to relax and soak in Nuremberg's local vibe.

Location: Obere Wörthstraße 10, 90403 Nuremberg

Must-try: Homemade quiches and daily pasta specials

5. Heilig-Geist-Spital

Located along the Pegnitz River, Heilig-Geist-Spital offers a blend of historical architecture and traditional Franconian dishes. Originally a medieval hospital, this restaurant serves regional specialties in a picturesque setting, including hearty stews, roasts, and seasonal dishes. Dining here is like stepping back in time, and the riverside terrace offers stunning views. It's a perfect spot for a cozy dinner with a touch of Nuremberg's storied past.

Location: Spitalgasse 16, 90403 Nuremberg

Must-try: Franconian Sauerbraten (marinated pot roast) with red cabbage and dumplings

6. Restauration Kopernikus

Located in the historic Katharinenkloster ruins, Restauration Kopernikus offers a distinctive experience with its Polish-inspired cuisine. Known for its beautiful architecture and serene courtyard, this restaurant focuses on Polish specialties with a German twist, making it an interesting option for those seeking a change from traditional German dishes. The atmosphere is warm and welcoming, providing a cozy setting that reflects the unique blend of cultures.

Location: Am Katharinenkloster 6, 90403 Nuremberg

Must-try: Pierogi (Polish dumplings) with various fillings and smoked trout salad

7. Alte Küchn'n & Im Keller

For a medieval dining experience, head to Alte Küchn'n & Im Keller, where rustic decor and historic recipes bring Nuremberg's culinary past to life. Known for its large portions and traditional Franconian fare, this restaurant's cellar dining area offers a unique atmosphere. The menu includes favorites like pork knuckle, schnitzel, and local beers. It's a great choice for a relaxed dinner in an authentic, old-world setting.

Location: Albrecht-Dürer-Straße 3, 90403 Nuremberg

Must-try: Pork knuckle with potato salad and Franconian beer

8. Zum Gulden Stern

Recognized as the oldest bratwurst restaurant in the world, Zum Gulden Stern has been serving Nürnberger bratwurst since the 14th century. This quaint, historic spot grills its sausages over an open flame, giving them a distinctive flavor. The simple, time-honored menu lets the quality of ingredients shine, making it a popular spot for both locals and visitors alike.

Location: Zirkelschmiedsgasse 26, 90402 Nuremberg

Must-try: Nürnberger bratwurst with potato salad or sauerkraut

Final Tips for Dining in Nuremberg

Nuremberg's restaurants often emphasize seasonality and local ingredients, so dishes may vary depending on when you visit. Reservations are recommended for the more popular or upscale spots, especially on weekends. And don't forget to pair your meals with regional

wines or Franconian beers to enjoy the full Nuremberg dining experience!

6.3 CAFÉS AND BAKERIES

Nuremberg is a delightful destination for café culture enthusiasts and pastry lovers, with a broad selection of cozy spots and bakeries offering both traditional and innovative flavors. Here's a guide to some of the most recommended cafés and bakeries around the city:

1. Traditional German Bakeries

Lebkuchen Schmidt

Location: Hauptmarkt

Specialties: Lebkuchen, Bavarian pastries, seasonal treats

Known for its authentic Nuremberg Lebkuchen (gingerbread), Lebkuchen Schmidt is a must-visit. This historic bakery has been producing these spiced, nutty delights for over a century. Their traditional Christmas Lebkuchen are packed with rich flavors of honey, nuts, and spices, making them perfect souvenirs or a treat to enjoy with coffee. They also offer a variety of Bavarian pastries, cakes, and seasonal baked goods that reflect the local traditions.

Der Beck

Location: Multiple locations around the city

As one of the most popular chains in Nuremberg, Der Beck offers a great selection of German baked goods, including pretzels, rolls, and fruit-studded cakes. Their seasonal pastries, like marzipan-filled sweets in winter and fruit tarts in summer, are particularly well-loved by locals. Der Beck locations are easy to spot around the city, providing an accessible taste of authentic German baking at any time of day.

2. Contemporary Cafés with a Twist

Café Bar Katz

Location: Bauerngasse
Specialties: Specialty coffee, vegan cakes, hearty breakfasts

Café Bar Katz is a welcoming space for those looking for quality coffee and a creative atmosphere. Known for its artisan brews, it's popular among locals and travelers alike. They offer a variety of vegan and gluten-free treats, from rich cakes to wholesome breakfast bowls. With its friendly vibe and trendy decor, it's an ideal spot to relax, enjoy a coffee, and try something a bit out of the ordinary in Nuremberg.

Machhörndl Kaffee

Location: Findelgasse and further locations
Specialties: Espresso-based drinks, pour-overs, sustainable practices

If you're a coffee connoisseur, Machhörndl Kaffee is a must. They are celebrated for their dedication to sourcing high-quality beans and practicing sustainable roasting. With expertly crafted espresso drinks and pour-overs, this café serves some of the best coffee in the city. Their minimalist design and skilled baristas make it a great place for savoring an unhurried cup of coffee, accompanied by a small but refined selection of pastries.

3. Historic Cafés with Charm

Café Neef

Location: Winklerstraße
Specialties: Classic German cakes, pralines, handmade chocolates

Café Neef is a classic in Nuremberg's café scene, where you can immerse yourself in the city's confectionery heritage. Known for their elegant cakes, pastries, and pralines, they're particularly famous for Schwarzwälder Kirschtorte (Black Forest cake) and Esterházy slices, which are as beautiful as they are delicious. It's the perfect place to experience the charm of a traditional German café with a relaxing atmosphere and attentive service.

Back-Factory

Location: Ludwigstraße

While Back-Factory is a more modern concept, it has become a beloved stop for those looking to grab a quick bite. Known for its self-service setup and budget-friendly prices, it's ideal for a casual coffee and pastry experience. From freshly baked breads to savory snacks, it caters to all kinds of tastes, offering a practical and enjoyable experience in the heart of Nuremberg.

4. Unique Finds and Local Favorites

Tante Emma Laden & Café

Location: Peter-Vischer-Straße
Specialties: Quiches, homemade cakes, seasonal specialties

A charming blend of café and vintage store, Tante Emma Laden & Café has a unique atmosphere that sets it apart. Its quaint, retro decor is matched by a menu of homemade treats, including rich quiches, fresh salads, and a rotating selection of cakes that highlight seasonal ingredients. It's a cozy spot with a nostalgic vibe that invites you to slow down and enjoy a more intimate café experience.

Zeit & Raum Café

Location: Äußerer Laufer Platz
Specialties: International flavors, brunch, fresh pastries

Zeit & Raum offers a laid-back atmosphere that's ideal for brunch or a late breakfast. The café is known for its international-inspired menu, with dishes that range from French croissants to Italian paninis and Mediterranean salads. Their weekend brunches are particularly popular, so it's a great option if you're looking to mix traditional and international flavors in a lively and welcoming setting.

Tips for Visiting Nuremberg's Cafés and Bakeries

- **Timing Your Visit**: Most bakeries open early, making it easy to grab a morning pastry before exploring the city. However, some cafés get busy around midday, especially those with brunch options, so visiting earlier or later can help avoid crowds.

- **Trying Seasonal Specialties**:

Nuremberg's bakeries are well-known for seasonal offerings, especially during the winter holiday season. Don't miss the famous Lebkuchen or marzipan-filled treats that appear in the colder months.

- **Local Etiquette**: Many cafés have a relaxed vibe, but remember that tables are often self-cleared, so be mindful of returning dishes or trays when you're finished.

6.4 NIGHTLIFE OPTIONS: BARS AND CLUBS

Nuremberg's nightlife scene offers an impressive variety of experiences, from cozy bars to lively dance clubs, catering to diverse tastes and energy levels. Whether you're a fan of craft beer, cocktails, or dancing the night away, Nuremberg has you covered. Here's a guide to some of the best nightlife spots in the city.

Bars in Nuremberg

1. Mr. Kennedy's Speakeasy

Known for its unique 1920s vibe, Mr. Kennedy's is a hidden gem featuring a cozy, dimly lit atmosphere and a selection of creative cocktails. With a focus on mixology, this speakeasy is ideal for those looking to enjoy a sophisticated night out. Reservations are recommended due to limited seating.

2. Hausbrauerei Altstadthof

A classic choice for beer lovers, Hausbrauerei Altstadthof brews its own beer using traditional Franconian methods. It's located near the Kaiserburg Castle, making it a popular stop for visitors interested in tasting regional specialties. Try their house-made red beer, which is an iconic local favorite.

3. Bar Nürnberg

Situated in the heart of Nuremberg, Bar Nürnberg combines a sleek, modern interior with an extensive drink menu. Their cocktail list is especially notable, featuring both classic and experimental drinks. With a lively atmosphere, it's a great place to start your night before heading to nearby clubs.

4. Bruderherz Brewery

Located near the Old Town, Bruderherz Brewery is a trendy brewery and bar in one. Known for its cozy yet vibrant atmosphere, the brewery offers a fantastic selection of freshly brewed beers, with some seasonal rotations. It's a perfect spot to enjoy a craft beer in a casual setting.

5. Bar Celona Nuremberg

A popular destination with a lively ambiance, Bar Celona serves tapas alongside its creative cocktails, making it ideal for a pre-club snack. With Spanish-inspired decor and a spacious outdoor terrace, it's a fun, relaxed spot for groups and casual gatherings.

Clubs in Nuremberg

1. Mach1 Club

One of the city's most iconic clubs, Mach1 is known for its electrifying atmosphere, pulsing beats, and international DJ lineup. Located near the city center, Mach1 features multiple dance floors and a wide variety of music genres, from electronic and house to hip-hop. It's popular with a younger crowd and perfect for those looking to dance until the early hours.

2. Club Stereo

Club Stereo is a favorite among locals, especially those who enjoy indie and alternative music. This intimate club attracts a slightly older crowd, offering live bands and themed DJ nights. It's a more low-key, eclectic environment compared to the mainstream club scene, but it's a great choice for music lovers seeking something different.

3. Die Rakete

Die Rakete is a renowned electronic music club that's well known across Germany for its cutting-edge techno scene. With its high-quality sound system, Die Rakete hosts both local and international DJs and is considered a must-visit for electronic music enthusiasts. Expect a high-energy crowd and a dance floor that stays full until morning.

4. Indabahn

Located in a former train station, Indabahn is a unique club with an industrial-chic interior. The club's music ranges from hip-hop to electro, and it's popular for its theme nights and special events. The atmosphere is vibrant and a bit more upscale, attracting both locals and tourists alike.

5. Club Goija

An upscale club with an exclusive vibe, Club Goija is known for its chic decor and premium drink offerings. It often features guest DJs playing popular dance tracks, and the dress code tends to be more formal. If you're looking for a more glamorous night out, Club Goija is a top choice.

Tips for Enjoying Nuremberg's Nightlife

- **Timing**: Most bars in Nuremberg get busy around 8–10 PM, while clubs usually open their doors around 11 PM and stay open until 4 or 5 AM.

- **Transportation**:

Taxis and rideshares are available, but the city's public transit system is efficient and runs late into the night, making it easy to get around.

- **Dress Codes**: While bars are generally casual, some clubs, especially upscale venues like Club Goija, enforce a dress code. Smart-casual attire is usually a safe choice.

- **Local Etiquette**: Remember that tipping in Germany is customary but modest (around 10%). Additionally, it's common for bars to serve a glass of water on request with your drink, which can be helpful if you're pacing yourself for a night out.

7.0 SHOPPING IN NUREMBERG

7.1 BEST AREAS FOR SHOPPING

Nuremberg is a treasure trove for shoppers, offering a unique blend of traditional craftsmanship, contemporary boutiques, and vibrant shopping streets. From medieval marketplaces to modern malls, there's something for everyone. Here are some of the best areas to shop and immerse yourself in the city's unique retail culture.

1. Karolinenstraße – The Main Shopping Boulevard

Karolinenstraße is Nuremberg's most popular shopping street, bustling with energy and lined with well-known brands, department stores, and specialty shops. Here, you'll find everything from high-street fashion to electronic gadgets and cosmetics. Stores like H&M, Zara, and MediaMarkt make it a go-to spot for both tourists and locals. This pedestrian-friendly street offers a lively atmosphere, with cafés and street performers adding to the shopping experience. Don't miss the seasonal decorations if you're visiting around Christmas!

2. Breite Gasse – Fashion and Footwear Haven

For those seeking fashion, Breite Gasse is a must-visit. Known for its impressive selection of clothing and shoe stores, this area houses popular European brands like Mango, Deichmann, and Esprit. The variety here suits a range of styles and budgets, making it easy to find something that suits your taste. Breite Gasse also offers various accessory shops and small boutiques, ideal for picking up unique pieces to remember your trip by.

3. Weißgerbergasse – Boutique Shopping with a Medieval Twist

Step back in time along Weißgerbergasse, Nuremberg's picturesque medieval street. With its half-timbered houses and charming cobblestone path, this street is filled with artisanal shops and independent boutiques. Look for handmade jewelry, one-of-a-kind crafts, and art galleries that showcase local talent. It's a quieter, more intimate shopping experience, offering items that reflect the history and culture of Nuremberg. This area is perfect for finding gifts or souvenirs with a true Nuremberg touch.

4. Kaiserstraße – Luxury Shopping District

If luxury brands and exclusive items are what you're after, Kaiserstraße is the place to be.

Known for its high-end boutiques and elegant storefronts, this area features premium brands such as Gucci, Prada, and Louis Vuitton. Kaiserstraße's upscale vibe attracts shoppers looking for designer fashion, fine jewelry, and quality leather goods. While prices here are premium, the service and selection are exceptional, ensuring a memorable shopping experience for those seeking a bit of indulgence.

5. Handwerkerhof – Traditional Crafts Market

Located near Nuremberg's main train station, Handwerkerhof (Craftsmen's Courtyard) offers a step into the past with its medieval-style marketplace dedicated to traditional German craftsmanship. Inside, you'll find artisans selling everything from hand-carved wooden toys and Christmas decorations to delicate pottery and leather goods. This is a must-see for those looking to buy authentic Nuremberg souvenirs, especially during the holiday season when the ambiance is enhanced with festive decorations and seasonal treats.

6.   Shopping   at   Nuremberg's Christkindlesmarkt (Christmas Market)

One of the most iconic Christmas markets in the world, Nuremberg's Christkindlesmarkt is an unmissable shopping destination if you visit during the holiday season. Held in the Hauptmarkt square, this historic market features hundreds of stalls offering traditional holiday items, from handcrafted ornaments and candles to sweets like gingerbread and roasted almonds.

Shopping at Christkindlesmarkt is a sensory experience with sights, sounds, and smells that evoke holiday nostalgia. It's the ideal place to pick up unique gifts and festive decorations.

7. Franken-Center – The Modern Shopping Mall

For a more contemporary shopping experience, head to the Franken-Center in Nuremberg's southern district of Langwasser. This large shopping mall has over 100 stores, including popular German and international retailers like

C&A, Saturn, and Müller. Offering a convenient mix of fashion, electronics, and dining options, it's a great one-stop destination for those looking to spend a day shopping indoors. Its family-friendly setup and variety of stores make it a perfect choice for all ages.

8. Vintage Shopping and Thrift Stores

Nuremberg also has a growing vintage and secondhand shopping scene for the environmentally conscious or those seeking unique finds. Stores like Vintage & Rags and Kleidermarkt offer a curated selection of pre-loved clothing, accessories, and quirky items. Each piece has a story, making it an interesting alternative to mainstream fashion. Thrift stores in the area often feature rare collectibles, retro styles, and gently used items, perfect for shoppers on a budget or anyone looking for something distinctive.

7.2 LOCAL SOUVENIRS AND CRAFTS

Nuremberg offers a delightful variety of souvenirs and crafts that capture the essence of the city's rich history, cultural heritage, and traditional craftsmanship. From handcrafted items that celebrate the region's medieval roots to local delicacies you can enjoy at home, Nuremberg's souvenirs are perfect for keeping memories alive or sharing a piece of your journey with loved ones. Here are some quintessential Nuremberg souvenirs that will bring the charm of this historic city back with you.

1. Nuremberg Gingerbread (Lebkuchen)

Perhaps Nuremberg's most famous edible souvenir, Lebkuchen, or gingerbread, has been a local specialty for over 600 years. Traditionally crafted by guild bakers using honey, nuts, spices, and other natural ingredients, Nuremberg Lebkuchen is an official Protected Geographical Indication (PGI) product, ensuring its authenticity. During the holiday season, you can find these delicious treats at the Christkindlesmarkt (Nuremberg Christmas Market), sold in beautifully decorated tins that make perfect gifts. There are several types, including soft Elisenlebkuchen with a high nut content and the crisp Oblaten-Lebkuchen baked on thin wafers.

2. Handcrafted Toys and Wooden Crafts

Nuremberg has a long tradition of toy-making, dating back to the Middle Ages. The city was once known as the "Toy Capital of the World," a legacy celebrated today in the many toy shops and the German Toy Museum. Visitors can purchase exquisite handcrafted wooden toys, dolls, puzzles, and models made with exceptional attention to detail. Many of these toys are inspired by traditional German folk art, and local workshops even offer miniature replicas of famous Nuremberg landmarks, ideal for bringing home a piece of the city's architectural charm.

3. Nutcrackers and Smokers

A symbol of German holiday traditions, nutcrackers are widely available in Nuremberg and make for charming keepsakes. These intricately designed figurines are often crafted by local artisans and range from small, simple designs to larger, more detailed models. Smokers, which are small incense burners often crafted in whimsical shapes like traditional Bavarian figures or winter scenes, are another popular choice, especially around the holiday season. Both items reflect the region's folklore and festive spirit, making them perfect for decorating your home or sharing as gifts.

4. Beer Steins and Traditional Glassware

312

Bavaria, where Nuremberg is located, is famous for its beer culture, and no visit would be complete without a souvenir beer stein. These steins, often handcrafted from stoneware and decorated with regional motifs, are both functional and collectible. Many feature pewter lids and elaborate carvings depicting Bavarian landscapes, local landmarks, or historic figures. For something unique, visit a local shop where artisans personalize steins with custom engravings. Additionally, Nuremberg's traditional glassware includes fine crystal pieces and delicate glasses etched with Bavarian themes, perfect for beer, wine, or schnapps.

5. Hand-Painted Christmas Ornaments

Nuremberg's Christmas markets are famous for their beautifully crafted holiday decorations. The city is home to countless artisans who create hand-painted glass ornaments, wooden tree decorations, and delicate figurines that add a festive touch to any holiday decor. Some ornaments are adorned with winter scenes of Nuremberg's Old Town or representations of its iconic landmarks, making them unique souvenirs that capture the spirit of the season. If you visit during the Christmas season, take advantage of the opportunity to watch artisans at work in their stalls and pick out ornaments as one-of-a-kind keepsakes.

6. Local Pottery and Ceramics

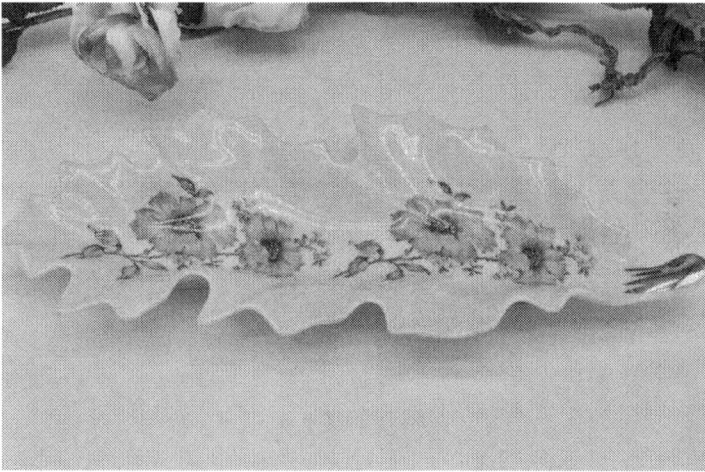

Nuremberg boasts a range of distinctive ceramics crafted by skilled artisans. Local pottery often features rich colors and intricate designs inspired by Bavarian folk art. Ceramic mugs, plates, and decorative bowls make excellent souvenirs and can serve as functional pieces at home. Look for items with traditional German motifs, such as floral patterns, wildlife, or Bavarian landscapes, all hand-painted by local craftsmen. Some shops even offer custom designs, allowing you to bring home a personalized memento of your trip.

7. Nuremberg Sausage and Mustard

Nuremberg's culinary heritage is well-known, and food items like Nuremberg sausages and mustard make great edible souvenirs. Nuremberg sausages, known for their small size and flavorful seasoning, are often packaged in vacuum-sealed containers that make them travel-friendly. Pair them with jars of traditional mustard, available in various flavors from mild to spicy. Many local delis and specialty stores offer gift boxes that combine these ingredients for a complete culinary experience you can recreate at home.

8. Handmade Jewelry and Metal Crafts

The medieval craft of metalworking is still alive in Nuremberg, with artisans creating beautiful jewelry and decorative pieces from silver, brass, and other metals. Many items reflect Nuremberg's Gothic and Renaissance influences, including rings, pendants, and bracelets with intricate designs. In addition to jewelry, you'll also find handcrafted metal souvenirs such as miniature swords, shields, or small replicas of medieval armor, inspired by the city's historic role as a center for weapon-making. These items are ideal for history enthusiasts or anyone seeking a unique piece of local artistry.

9. Art Prints and Local Paintings

NUREMBERG
GERMANY

For art lovers, Nuremberg offers various galleries and shops featuring prints and paintings that capture the city's medieval charm. Many artists are inspired by Nuremberg's half-timbered houses, Gothic churches, and iconic landmarks, producing works in styles ranging from detailed realism to impressionistic interpretations. Smaller prints and sketches are easy to carry and make wonderful gifts, while larger pieces can be professionally packaged for travel. These artworks make for an elegant way to bring Nuremberg's beauty into your home.

10. Handmade Candles

Nuremberg's candle-making tradition is another craft that makes for a memorable souvenir. Locally made candles are often shaped into holiday motifs, decorated with Bavarian patterns, or scented with traditional German spices like cinnamon and clove. You can find everything from elegant taper candles to rustic pillar candles with a handmade touch, perfect for adding a cozy feel to your home or as a thoughtful gift.

7.3 MARKETS AND BAZAARS

Nuremberg is famous for its lively markets, where visitors can experience the authentic flavors, crafts, and culture of Bavaria. Whether you're a food lover, a fan of handmade goods, or just looking for a unique souvenir, Nuremberg's markets offer an array of options throughout the year. Here's a closer look at some of the must-visit markets and bazaars.

Hauptmarkt (Main Market Square)

Located in the heart of Nuremberg's Old Town, Hauptmarkt is the city's central marketplace and a focal point for locals and tourists alike. Here, vendors sell fresh produce, meats, cheeses, and regional delicacies, offering a true taste of Franconian cuisine. Hauptmarkt is also famous for its daily operations, making it a great spot to pick up essentials or simply immerse yourself in the daily life of Nuremberg. The square is also surrounded by impressive landmarks, including the ornate Schöner Brunnen fountain and the Frauenkirche, adding to the atmosphere of the market.

Christkindlesmarkt (Nuremberg Christmas Market)

One of Germany's oldest and most beloved Christmas markets, the Christkindlesmarkt is an essential part of the Nuremberg holiday experience. Held in Hauptmarkt, the Christkindlesmarkt transforms the square into a festive wonderland each Advent season. Wooden stalls adorned with holiday decorations sell everything from handcrafted ornaments to mulled wine (Glühwein) and the famous

Nürnberger Lebkuchen (gingerbread). There's also a special section for children, complete with a carousel and kid-friendly activities, making this market a family favorite. As evening falls, the twinkling lights and aromas of roasted nuts and spices make for an unforgettable winter experience.

Handwerkerhof (Craftsmen's Courtyard)

Nestled near Nuremberg's medieval city walls, Handwerkerhof transports visitors back in time with its cobblestone paths and half-timbered houses. This quaint artisan market is home to skilled craftsmen selling handmade items, including pottery, jewelry, leather goods, and traditional Franconian crafts. Handwerkerhof is particularly popular during the warmer months, but it's also a cozy winter spot, as many artisans open their workshops to visitors. This is a fantastic place to watch local artisans at work, gain insight into traditional craft methods, and purchase one-of-a-kind souvenirs.

Wochenmarkt (Weekly Market)

For a more local, everyday experience, head to one of Nuremberg's weekly markets. These smaller markets are scattered throughout various neighborhoods, often held in local squares, and typically feature fresh fruits, vegetables, flowers, and baked goods. Popular spots include the market in Maxfeld and the farmers' market at Königstor, where vendors bring goods directly from nearby farms. Here, you'll have the chance to interact with locals and sample seasonal produce at reasonable prices. It's an ideal setting to learn about Bavarian agriculture and enjoy the community spirit.

Flea Markets and Antiques

Nuremberg is also a hub for antique lovers and bargain hunters. The Trempelmarkt, one of Germany's largest flea markets, is held twice a year and offers everything from vintage furniture and collectibles to rare books and curiosities. Walking through the Trempelmarkt feels like embarking on a treasure hunt, with hundreds of vendors selling items that range from nostalgic to valuable. Another popular spot for antiques is the antique fair held in Hauptmarkt, where you can find a variety of authentic Bavarian artifacts and quirky finds.

Seasonal Markets

Beyond the Christmas season, Nuremberg hosts several other seasonal markets worth visiting. The Easter Market, or Ostermarkt, takes place in spring, featuring Easter-themed crafts, decorations, and candies. In autumn, Nuremberg hosts the Kirchweih market, where locals celebrate with food stalls, beer, and live entertainment in honor of the church consecration. These seasonal markets add a unique dimension to the city's calendar and offer insight into the local customs and traditions that shape Nuremberg's cultural identity.

Tips for Visiting Nuremberg's Markets

- **Timing**: Arrive early to beat the crowds, especially during weekends or festive events.

- **Cash**: Many vendors prefer cash, so having some on hand will make transactions smoother.

- **Try the Local Specialties**:

Don't miss the chance to sample Nürnberger Rostbratwurst (grilled sausages), regional cheeses, and local pastries.

- **Ask for Recommendations**: Vendors are often friendly and eager to share tips on the best local products or hidden gems in the city.

8.0 OUTDOOR ACTIVITIES

8.1 PARKS AND GREEN SPACES

Nuremberg, a city celebrated for its medieval charm, also brims with lush green spaces that offer tranquil escapes from the bustling city. Whether you're seeking a peaceful stroll, an engaging day out with family, or a deeper connection with nature, Nuremberg's parks are rich in history, beauty, and recreation. Here's a look at some must-visit parks and green spaces.

1. Tiergarten Nuremberg (Nuremberg Zoo)

Nestled within the verdant landscape of the Schmausenbuck hill, Tiergarten is more than just a zoo; it's a nature lover's paradise. Covering over 67 hectares, this expansive area is home to around 300 species of animals, including rare creatures like Siberian tigers, manatees, and dolphins. The zoo's unique feature is its blend of natural surroundings with the animal habitats, creating an immersive experience for visitors. With shaded walking paths and picnic spots, it's a perfect family-friendly destination.

Highlights: Dolphin lagoon, large playgrounds, and seasonal events.

2. Volkspark Marienberg

Located in the northern part of Nuremberg, Volkspark Marienberg is a local favorite for sports and leisure. The park covers over 90

hectares and offers extensive biking and walking trails, fitness stations, sports fields, and areas for rollerblading. The beautifully landscaped garden area and the large ponds provide a picturesque setting for relaxation. During summer, you'll find locals enjoying barbecues or picnics in designated areas, creating a lively yet peaceful atmosphere.

Highlights: Barbecue spots, sports facilities, and an open-air stage for events.

3. Hesperidengarten

For those seeking a slice of elegance, the Hesperidengarten is a hidden gem in Nuremberg's St. Johannis district. Modeled after the 17th-century Renaissance gardens, it features beautifully designed flower beds, fountains, and sculptures. Originally, this garden was created to showcase rare plants and herbs, and its legacy continues with an assortment of botanical varieties. Visitors will enjoy the serene ambiance, making it a lovely spot for contemplation or an afternoon read.

Highlights: Renaissance design, rare plants, and artistic sculptures.

4. Wöhrder Wiese

A green oasis along the Pegnitz River, Wöhrder Wiese is a popular spot for both locals and tourists. With expansive meadows, vibrant flower beds, and plenty of benches, this park is ideal for a leisurely afternoon or a relaxing walk. The picturesque paths along the river are perfect for jogging or cycling, while the play areas make it a hit among families. In warmer months,

Wöhrder Wiese hosts various events and outdoor performances, adding a lively touch to this riverside retreat.

Highlights: Riverside paths, family-friendly play areas, and seasonal festivals.

5. Luitpoldhain

Luitpoldhain is a historical park with a unique charm. Known for its beautiful open spaces and lush greenery, it was originally designed as a memorial park. Today, it's a popular gathering place, particularly for music lovers, as it hosts open-air concerts, including the renowned

Klassik Open Air concerts. The park's large, open fields and shaded walking paths make it ideal for a relaxed afternoon, whether you're interested in a picnic, a leisurely walk, or simply soaking in the park's tranquil vibe.

Highlights: Klassik Open Air concerts, spacious lawns, and shaded paths.

6. Reichswald Forest

For travelers looking for a more extensive exploration of nature, the Reichswald Forest on the outskirts of Nuremberg is a vast area perfect for hiking and immersing oneself in natural beauty. This historic forest has a network of trails suited for all levels, along with dedicated picnic areas and quiet nooks to escape the city's hustle. Its dense woods, varied terrain, and abundant wildlife make it an excellent spot for nature lovers and hikers alike.

Highlights: Hiking trails, wildlife spotting, and extensive forested areas.

7. Westpark

Located in the western part of Nuremberg, Westpark is a modern green space that appeals to all ages. Opened in 2004, it offers well-maintained paths, spacious lawns, playgrounds, and interactive water features, making it especially popular among families with children. Its design reflects a blend of traditional and contemporary elements, with manicured flower beds, an amphitheater, and tranquil spots for unwinding.

Highlights: Children's play areas, modern design, and a summer splash zone.

8. Dutzendteich Park

Dutzendteich Park is a picturesque lakeside park offering plenty of scenic spots and recreational activities. The large lake is perfect for boating, while the surrounding paths are ideal for cycling and jogging. Located near the historical Nazi Party Rally Grounds, Dutzendteich also offers visitors a chance to learn about Germany's history alongside enjoying nature. It's a favorite among both locals and tourists, especially during spring and summer when the park's natural beauty is in full bloom.

Highlights: Boat rentals, lakeside picnicking, and historical significance.

Tips for Enjoying Nuremberg's Green Spaces

- **Plan for Picnics**:

Many parks in Nuremberg offer designated barbecue areas and open fields perfect for a picnic. Pack some local snacks and enjoy a relaxed meal amidst nature.

- **Check Events**:

Parks like Luitpoldhain and Wöhrder Wiese often host events and festivals. Check the local listings to catch open-air concerts, theater performances, or seasonal festivities.

- **Family-Friendly Spots**: For families with children, parks like Westpark and Tiergarten provide play areas and interactive zones to keep kids entertained.

- **Stay Active**: Bring along a bike, skates, or even a frisbee. Nuremberg's parks are well-suited for a range of outdoor activities, from jogging to biking.

8.2 WALKING AND CYCLING ROUTES

Nuremberg offers a blend of historic charm and scenic beauty, making it ideal for exploring on foot or by bike. This guide outlines some of the best routes to experience the city, with options for casual strolls, invigorating walks, and enjoyable cycling paths.

1. Old Town Walking Tour

Distance: Approximately 3 km
Time: 2-3 hours at a leisurely pace
Difficulty: Easy

This classic route through Nuremberg's Old Town takes you through the heart of the city's historical landmarks, showcasing its medieval architecture and rich heritage.

- **Starting Point**: Begin at the Hauptmarkt (Main Market Square), home to the beautiful Frauenkirche (Church of Our

Lady) and the Schöner Brunnen (Beautiful Fountain).

- **Highlights**: Walk through the charming squares, past Albrecht Dürer's House, and head towards the Imperial Castle, where you'll enjoy panoramic views of the city.

- **Ending Point**: The route concludes at the Handwerkerhof, a medieval-style crafts village where you can enjoy traditional food and handmade souvenirs.

This route is perfect for history lovers who want to immerse themselves in Nuremberg's past and is a relatively short walk suitable for all fitness levels.

2. The Pegnitz Riverside Path

Distance: 5 km round-trip
Time: 1.5-2 hours
Difficulty: Moderate

This path along the Pegnitz River is one of Nuremberg's hidden gems, providing a peaceful escape with stunning river views, lush greenery, and small bridges that enhance the scenic atmosphere.

- **Starting Point**: Start near Kettensteg, an old iron bridge known for its historic appeal.

- **Highlights**: Follow the river eastward, passing picturesque parks and green spaces like the Wöhrder Wiese. The path has plenty of benches and picnic areas for breaks.

- **Ending Point**: The turnaround point is the Wöhrder See, a serene lake where you can rest, have a picnic, or continue exploring.

The Pegnitz Riverside Path is perfect for those seeking a relaxing stroll away from the city center's hustle and bustle.

3. The Nuremberg Ring Cycle Route

Distance: 50 km loop
Time: 4-5 hours by bike
Difficulty: Moderate to challenging

The Nuremberg Ring Cycle Route is ideal for cyclists eager to explore the city and its surrounding neighborhoods in depth. This circular path offers a balanced mix of urban and natural scenery, taking you through parks, along rivers, and around Nuremberg's outskirts.

- **Starting Point**: Begin at the Dutzendteich Lake in the southeast part of the city.

- **Highlights**: Cycle past the Reichsparteitagsgelände (former Nazi Party Rally Grounds), through picturesque parks like the Volkspark Marienberg, and onto suburban trails that offer a glimpse into Nuremberg's residential areas.

- **Ending Point**: The route completes the loop back at Dutzendteich Lake, where you can relax or enjoy some lakeside activities.

This extensive route is ideal for avid cyclists looking for a full-day adventure and provides a comprehensive look at both Nuremberg's history and natural surroundings.

4. City Parks and Gardens Walk

Distance: 4 km
Time: 1.5-2 hours
Difficulty: Easy

This gentle route connects some of Nuremberg's loveliest parks, perfect for nature enthusiasts and those looking for a leisurely walk among greenery.

- Starting Point: Start at the Rosenau Park, known for its blooming flowers and shaded paths.

- Highlights: Walk to the Hallerwiese, a riverside park with open lawns and play areas. Continue towards the Cramer-Klett-Park, famous for its peaceful ponds and lush landscapes.

- Ending Point: End at Wöhrder Wiese, where you can enjoy the beautiful views along the Pegnitz River.

This route is well-suited for those wanting a relaxing outing, perfect for families or solo travelers who appreciate green spaces.

5. The Medieval City Walls Walk

Distance: 5 km
Time: 1-2 hours
Difficulty: Moderate

A unique way to see Nuremberg is by walking along its medieval city walls. This route takes you along the well-preserved sections, offering an immersive experience in the city's history.

- **Starting Point**: Begin at the Königstor Gate, an impressive entry point into the old town.

- **Highlights**: Follow the walls, passing towers and gateways like the Tiergärtnertor, with great views of the cityscape. Look out for interpretive signs along the way explaining the walls' history.

- **Ending Point**: The walk ends at the Frauentor, a bustling area filled with shops and cafes.

This route is a must for history buffs, offering insights into Nuremberg's past defenses and architecture.

Practical Tips for Walking and Cycling in Nuremberg

- **Navigation**:

Maps and information boards are
available at major sites. Downloadable
maps are also available for specific routes.

- **Safety**: All paths are well-maintained, but
  cyclists should watch out for pedestrians
  in shared spaces.

- **Rental Options**: Bicycles are available
  for rent at multiple locations throughout
  the city, including e-bikes for longer
  routes.

- **Seasons**: Spring and autumn offer mild weather, ideal for both walking and cycling, while winter provides a unique atmosphere for those interested in a quieter experience.

8.3 DAY TRIPS FROM NUREMBERG

Nuremberg is not only a vibrant city with a rich history, but it's also a fantastic gateway to some of Bavaria's most charming and historically significant towns. Here are several destinations perfect for day trips from Nuremberg, each offering its own unique attractions, landscapes, and cultural experiences.

1. Bamberg

Travel Time: Approximately 1 hour by train

Highlights: UNESCO World Heritage Sites, Old Town, Breweries

Bamberg is a beautifully preserved medieval town and a UNESCO World Heritage Site known for its scenic Old Town, picturesque canals, and unique Rauchbier (smoked beer). A walk through the historic heart of Bamberg reveals a mix of Gothic and baroque architecture, such as the Bamberg Cathedral, which houses the Bamberg Horseman sculpture, and the Alte Hofhaltung. Don't miss Little Venice, a cluster of quaint fisherman's houses along the Regnitz River. Bamberg's local breweries are a must-visit for a taste of the region's distinctive Rauchbier, especially popular with beer enthusiasts.

2. Rothenburg ob der Tauber

Travel Time: About 1.5 hours by car or 2 hours by train

Highlights: Medieval charm, Plönlein, Christmas Museum

Rothenburg ob der Tauber is perhaps Germany's most famous medieval town, with well-preserved half-timbered houses, cobblestone streets, and its iconic Plönlein (a picturesque square often photographed for its storybook beauty). Walk along the city walls, visit St. Jacob's Church to see the Holy Blood altarpiece, and explore the Medieval Crime Museum, which houses curious artifacts of justice from medieval times. If visiting around Christmas, the town becomes even more magical with the traditional Christmas market and the Käthe Wohlfahrt Christmas Museum, which operates year-round.

3. Regensburg

Travel Time: Around 1.5 hours by train

Highlights: Danube River, Roman ruins, Stone Bridge

Regensburg, another UNESCO World Heritage Site, is one of Germany's best-preserved medieval cities. Situated along the Danube River, Regensburg boasts attractions such as the Stone Bridge, which dates back to the 12th century, and St. Peter's Cathedral, a prime example of Gothic architecture. Stroll through the charming streets of the Old Town to admire the Roman and medieval architecture, with stops at the Roman Porta Praetoria and the Thurn und Taxis Palace. A boat ride along the Danube offers scenic views of this historical city from the water.

4. Bayreuth

Travel Time: About 1 hour by train

Highlights: Margravial Opera House, Wagner Festival, Hermitage Gardens

Bayreuth, famous for the annual Richard Wagner Festival, is home to the Margravial Opera House, a UNESCO World Heritage Site renowned for its baroque interiors. Tour the stunning Hermitage Palace and Gardens, a favorite summer retreat for nobility, and walk through the charming Old Town. If you're a fan of classical music, a visit to the Wagner Museum gives insight into the composer's life and legacy. Bayreuth offers a quieter, yet culturally rich day trip for travelers interested in music, art, and history.

5. Ansbach

Travel Time: Around 30 minutes by train

Highlights: Ansbach Residence, Rococo architecture, Hofgarten

Ansbach is a lesser-known yet delightful town with a rich history and beautiful Rococo architecture. The Ansbach Residence, the former seat of the Margraves of Brandenburg-Ansbach, is a highlight with its opulent state rooms and art collections. Take a stroll through the Hofgarten, a beautifully landscaped garden behind the palace, and enjoy the quiet charm of Ansbach's Old Town. It's a wonderful spot for those looking to escape larger tourist crowds while still experiencing Bavarian culture and history.

6. Würzburg

Travel Time: About 1 hour by train

Highlights: Würzburg Residence, Marienberg Fortress, vineyards

Würzburg is a Baroque gem nestled along the Main River, known for its exceptional wine and the UNESCO-listed Würzburg Residence, an architectural masterpiece with lavish interiors and gardens. Wander the historic Marienberg Fortress, perched on a hill with scenic views over the town, and cross the Old Main Bridge, lined with statues of saints. Wine lovers can visit local wineries for a taste of the region's celebrated Franconian wines, best enjoyed with a view of the vineyards rolling along the riverbanks.

7. Fränkische Schweiz (Franconian Switzerland)

Travel Time: About 1 hour by car

Highlights: Scenic landscapes, rock formations, hiking, caves

The Franconian Switzerland region, a favorite among nature lovers, is known for its unique rock formations, rolling hills, and charming villages. This area offers an abundance of outdoor activities such as hiking, rock climbing, and exploring stalactite caves like the Devil's

Cave in Pottenstein. Visitors can also enjoy the local breweries scattered throughout the region, as Franconian Switzerland boasts one of the highest concentrations of breweries in the world. With a car, you can leisurely tour the countryside, taking in the natural beauty and rural charm of Bavaria.

8. Dinkelsbühl

Travel Time: Around 1.5 hours by car

Highlights: Medieval walls, colorful town center, St. George's Minster

Often overshadowed by nearby Rothenburg ob der Tauber, Dinkelsbühl is equally enchanting but with fewer tourists. This well-preserved medieval town is encircled by fortified walls and filled with charming half-timbered houses in vibrant colors. Explore the town's quiet streets, visit St. George's Minster, and walk along the town walls to take in views of the surrounding countryside. Dinkelsbühl offers a peaceful retreat into medieval history and architecture, perfect for travelers seeking an authentic Bavarian experience away from the crowds.

9. Neuschwanstein Castle

Travel Time: Around 3 hours by car or train

Highlights: Iconic castle, panoramic views, fairy-tale architecture

While a bit further afield, a day trip to Neuschwanstein Castle is unforgettable. Known for its fairy-tale architecture, this 19th-century castle inspired Walt Disney's iconic castle and attracts visitors worldwide. Situated near the village of Hohenschwangau and surrounded by the Bavarian Alps, Neuschwanstein offers a stunning mix of architecture and natural beauty. Guided tours take you through King Ludwig II's luxurious chambers, offering insight into the king's eccentric life. Make sure to enjoy the breathtaking views from Marienbrücke (Mary's Bridge) for the best photo opportunities.

9.0 PRACTICAL INFORMATION

9.1 CURRENCY AND PAYMENT METHODS

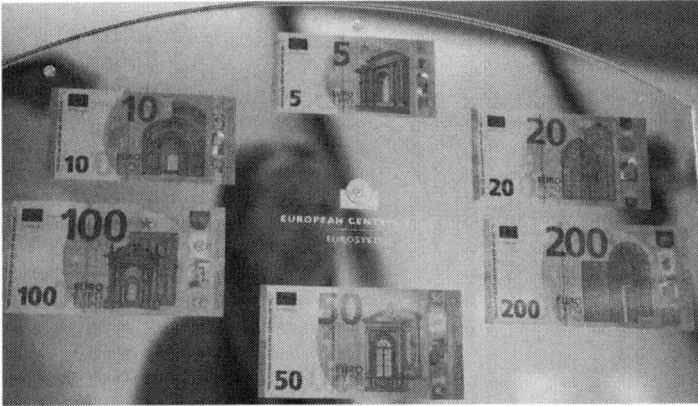

Nuremberg, like the rest of Germany, uses the Euro (€) as its official currency. The Euro is divided into 100 cents, and it comes in various denominations that are easy to familiarize yourself with before or upon arrival. Bills come in values of 5, 10, 20, 50, 100, 200, and 500 euros, while coins include 1 and 2 euros, as well as 1, 2, 5, 10, 20, and 50 cents. When traveling, having smaller denominations and a few coins on hand can be especially convenient for small purchases, tipping, or using public restrooms.

Cash vs. Card: What's Preferred?

While Germany has become more card-friendly in recent years, cash is still a widely used payment method in Nuremberg, especially in local shops, markets, and some smaller restaurants. German culture places a strong emphasis on privacy, which is one reason cash has remained popular. However, major retailers, hotels, and chain restaurants increasingly accept credit and debit cards, especially in urban areas like Nuremberg.

In Nuremberg's markets, such as the famous Christmas Market (Christkindlesmarkt), cash is generally preferred, though some vendors may now accept cards or contactless payment options. It's wise to carry some cash for smaller purchases or at venues where cards aren't accepted. ATMs are widely available throughout the city, making it convenient to withdraw euros as needed.

Credit and Debit Card Use

Visa and Mastercard are the most widely accepted credit and debit cards in Nuremberg. American Express and Discover cards are less common and might not be accepted at all locations. Before using your card, check with your bank regarding any foreign transaction fees to avoid surprises. Additionally, always carry a backup payment option, as some places may not take foreign-issued cards.

For card transactions, contactless payments (tap-to-pay) are becoming more common, especially at supermarkets, retail stores, and transportation services. However, it's essential to confirm with merchants whether they accept contactless payments, as some smaller businesses may still require a traditional card swipe or insert.

Mobile Payment Options

Germany has been somewhat slower to adopt mobile payments than some other European countries, but in larger cities like Nuremberg, you can use Apple Pay, Google Pay, and other mobile payment systems at many retail locations. Check with individual merchants about acceptance, as this option is more popular with younger consumers and major retailers. Be aware that mobile payments may not be accepted in more traditional or smaller establishments, especially outside the city center.

Tipping and Service Charges

In Germany, tipping isn't as customary as it is in some other countries, but it's always appreciated. Service charges are often included in the bill, especially at higher-end establishments, but it's polite to leave a small tip (about 5–10%) for good service, especially at restaurants, cafes, or with taxi drivers. If paying with cash, you can simply round up the total amount or give an additional euro or two. When tipping by card, be sure to inform the server of the tip amount before processing the payment, as it may not be possible to add a tip after the card has been swiped.

ATM Withdrawals and Fees

ATMs are plentiful in Nuremberg, and withdrawing cash is straightforward. Machines can be found in banks, shopping centers, and popular tourist areas. While most ATMs do not charge a usage fee, your bank may charge a foreign withdrawal fee, so it's a good idea to check with them ahead of time. If you have a travel-focused or international bank card, you may even be able to withdraw euros without additional charges.

Using ATMs within bank branches is recommended, as these are generally more secure and may have lower or no fees compared to stand-alone machines. Look for machines labeled "Geldautomat," which is the German term for ATMs.

Currency Exchange

While most travelers rely on ATMs, currency exchange services are available at the airport, major train stations, and certain areas in the city center. Exchange rates and fees vary, so it's wise to compare rates. Keep in mind that withdrawing from an ATM is often more favorable in terms of exchange rates than using currency exchange kiosks, though having some euros on hand before arriving can be useful.

Final Tips

- **Always carry some cash** for smaller, local purchases or tips.

- **Notify your bank** of your travel plans to avoid potential holds on your card.

- **Avoid carrying large amounts of cash** at once, for both convenience and security.

9.2 LANGUAGE AND COMMUNICATION

In Nuremberg, the official language is German, and you'll find that most locals speak German as their primary language. However, English is also widely spoken, especially among younger people, in popular tourist areas, hotels, restaurants, and museums. Here's what you should know to make your communication as smooth and enjoyable as possible during your trip.

Basic German Phrases

Learning a few basic German phrases can greatly enhance your experience and create positive connections with locals. Here are some essential phrases to help you get started:

- **Hello**: Hallo

- **Goodbye**: Auf Wiedersehen or Tschüss (informal)

- **Please**: Bitte

- **Thank you**: Danke

- **Excuse me**: Entschuldigung

- **Yes / No**: Ja / Nein

- **Do you speak English?** Sprechen Sie Englisch?

These simple phrases can be a great icebreaker and are often warmly received, even if your German isn't perfect. Showing an effort to speak the language is generally appreciated and often leads to more welcoming interactions.

Language Tools and Apps

While basic phrases are helpful, you may still encounter situations where you need a more in-depth understanding. Thankfully, language translation apps like Google Translate and iTranslate can assist in real time, helping you understand menus, signs, and other written materials. Many of these apps offer offline translation for German, which can be invaluable if you're in an area with limited internet access.

For travelers who prefer a digital approach, learning apps like Duolingo or Babbel can also help you pick up more German basics before or during your trip. They provide short, practical lessons focused on everyday vocabulary and phrases.

Signage and Navigation

Nuremberg's signage in tourist areas often includes English translations, especially in locations frequented by international travelers like the Old Town, museums, and the train stations. This makes navigating the city quite manageable for English-speaking visitors. However, outside the city center, you may find fewer English signs, so it's useful to have a basic understanding of German words related to transportation and directions:

- **Entrance**: Eingang

- **Exit**: Ausgang

- **Stop**: Halt

- **Restroom**: Toilette

- **Ticket**: Fahrkarte

- **Platform**: Gleis

Communicating in Restaurants and Shops

When dining out, English menus are common in central Nuremberg, particularly in restaurants that cater to tourists. Staff in these establishments often speak at least some English and are used to assisting visitors. If you venture into more local or traditional eateries, a German phrasebook or translation app will come in handy, especially for ordering and asking about ingredients if you have dietary restrictions.

In shops, many clerks and shop assistants will understand basic English, but it's polite to start interactions in German, even if only with a friendly "Hallo." If you're looking for a specific item, try using both German and English, or point to what you need if there's a language barrier. Generally, Nurembergers are friendly and willing to help, even if there's a bit of a language gap.

Cultural Tips for Communication

When engaging in conversation with locals, polite communication and respect for personal space are valued. Nuremberg residents often prefer a bit more formality, especially when meeting someone for the first time. Saying "Guten Tag" (Good day) or "Guten Abend" (Good evening) instead of a casual "Hallo" can show respect in these settings.

Understanding body language can also enhance your interactions. Germans typically appreciate a direct approach, and they're known for their straightforwardness. This might come across as formal to some, but it reflects a deep respect for clear and honest communication.

Emergency Communication and Assistance

In case of an emergency, most public officials, including police officers and hospital staff in Nuremberg, have a basic understanding of English. The nationwide emergency number in Germany is 112 for medical and fire emergencies and 110 for police assistance. Having these numbers saved and being able to convey basic information about your situation in German or English can be invaluable.

9.3 SAFETY TIPS

When traveling to Nuremberg, safety should always be a priority to ensure a smooth and enjoyable experience. While the city is generally safe for tourists, there are a few important guidelines to help you stay secure, especially if you're unfamiliar with the area or traveling for the first time.

1. Stay Aware of Your Surroundings

Like any major city, Nuremberg has busy areas where crowds can form, particularly in the old town or around tourist hotspots. Always be aware of your surroundings, especially in crowded places. Pickpockets can target tourists, particularly in busy markets like the Christkindlesmarkt (Nuremberg Christmas Market) or near major transportation hubs. Keep an eye on your belongings, and use a money belt or anti-theft bag for added security.

2. Use Public Transportation Safely

Nuremberg has an efficient public transportation system, including trams and buses, which are generally safe. However, late-night or early-morning travel can sometimes see fewer passengers, and it's always advisable to stay alert. Stick to well-lit, busy stations if you're traveling during off-peak hours. When using trams or buses, avoid leaving your personal items unattended.

3. Know the Emergency Numbers

In case of an emergency, it's important to know local emergency numbers. In Germany:

- Police: **110**

Ambulance/Fire: **112** Make sure to store these numbers in your phone and have them readily accessible.

4. Keep Your Passport and Valuables Secure

While Nuremberg is considered safe, petty theft can occur, especially in touristy areas. Keep your passport and other important documents in a hotel safe or a secure, hidden spot on your person. Avoid carrying too much cash and always carry a credit card or other secure form of payment.

5. Weather and Seasonal Considerations

Nuremberg experiences a range of weather conditions throughout the year, with cold winters and warm summers. Winter temperatures can dip below freezing, leading to icy sidewalks and potential slip hazards. Wear appropriate footwear, especially during the colder months. In the summer, stay hydrated and protect yourself from the sun, as Nuremberg can occasionally experience heatwaves.

6. Be Cautious with Alcohol Consumption

Nuremberg offers a variety of traditional beers and local drinks, but be mindful of your alcohol consumption. Public drinking is allowed, but excessive drinking can lead to accidents or uncomfortable situations, particularly in unfamiliar environments or when traveling alone. It's important to know your limits and always keep an eye on your drink to avoid any possible tampering.

7. Respect Local Laws and Customs

German laws are strict, and it's essential to follow them. Public drunkenness, inappropriate behavior, and disturbing the peace can lead to fines or legal issues. Nuremberg is known for its cultural heritage and historic sites, so showing respect to local customs and traditions, particularly in churches or sacred places, is appreciated.

8. Stay In Well-Lit, Busy Areas at Night

While Nuremberg is generally safe, like any city, some areas may be less populated and poorly lit after dark. Stick to well-lit streets and avoid wandering alone in secluded spots, especially at night. If you're unfamiliar with a neighborhood, research it in advance or ask locals for advice.

9. Travel Insurance

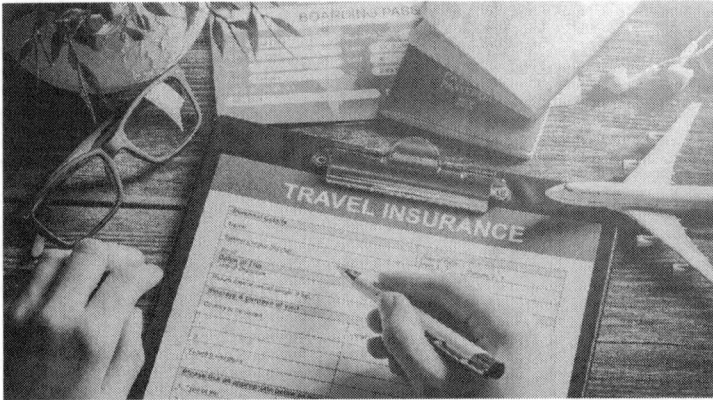

Before your trip, make sure to have comprehensive travel insurance that covers medical emergencies, trip cancellations, and lost luggage. In case of an accident or illness, healthcare can be expensive for non-residents, so it's best to have coverage for unexpected situations.

10. Cybersecurity

Public Wi-Fi networks are widely available in Nuremberg, but they can also be a target for hackers. Avoid accessing sensitive information, like bank accounts or credit card details, on unsecured networks. Use a virtual private network (VPN) if possible, and ensure your devices have updated security settings.

9.4 EMERGENCY CONTACTS

When traveling, it's essential to have quick access to emergency contacts. Here's a comprehensive list of numbers and resources for any emergency you might encounter while exploring Nuremberg. Keep this information handy, and if possible, save these numbers in your phone for quick access.

1. General Emergency Services: Police, Fire, and Medical Assistance

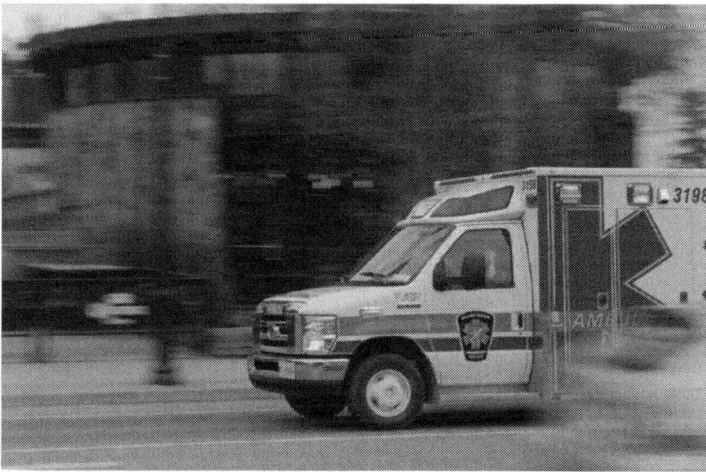

- **Universal Emergency Number (Police, Fire, Medical): 112**
  This is the European Union-wide emergency number. It connects you to dispatch for police, fire, or ambulance services. Operators usually speak English and can direct your call appropriately.

- **Police Emergency Number: 110**
  Directly connects you to the local police. Use this number for non-medical, non-fire emergencies, such as theft, vandalism, or personal safety issues. German police are known for their prompt response and professionalism.

2. Hospital and Medical Contacts

- **Nuremberg General Hospital (Klinikum Nürnberg):**

Phone: +49 911 398-0

Address: Prof.-Ernst-Nathan-Str. 1, 90419 Nuremberg

Klinikum Nürnberg is one of the main hospitals in the city and provides a range of medical services, including emergency care.

- **Nuremberg Children's Hospital (Kinderklinik Nürnberg):**

Phone: +49 911 393-2251

Address: Breslauer Str. 201, 90471 Nuremberg

For children's health emergencies, the Kinderklinik offers specialized care for younger patients.

- **Pharmacies (Apotheken) – Emergency Hours**

Nuremberg has an emergency pharmacy rotation. Outside regular hours, pharmacies display the details of the nearest open location. Alternatively, you can call **+49 800 0022833** to find the nearest available pharmacy.

3. Travel Assistance and Embassy Contacts

- **Tourist Emergency Hotline**
  Phone: +49 911 23360
  This is a helpline for tourists, operated by the local tourist office. They can provide assistance or advice in various situations, including non-emergencies, lost property, or general guidance.

- **Your Country's Embassy or Consulate**
  If you face legal issues, lose your passport, or need assistance from your country's authorities, contact your nearest embassy or consulate. Many embassies in Berlin or Munich can assist travelers in Nuremberg. Be sure to have the contact information for your country's embassy before traveling.

4. Mental Health and Crisis Helplines

- **Mental Health Support Hotline**
  Phone: +49 800 1110111
  This free, 24/7 hotline provides support for those dealing with mental health concerns, stress, or any personal crisis. Support is available in multiple languages.

- **Women's Crisis Helpline**
  Phone: +49 911 529191
  This helpline offers confidential support for women dealing with harassment or violence. There are also shelters and counseling centers across the city.

5. Roadside Assistance

- **ADAC (Allgemeiner Deutscher Automobil-Club)**

Phone: +49 89 20 20 4000

ADAC provides assistance for breakdowns, accidents, and vehicle-related emergencies. They can also arrange towing and repair services.

Tips for Emergency Situations in Nuremberg

- **Language Barrier**:

While many emergency operators speak English, it can help to know a few German phrases or have a translation app handy.

- **Identify Landmarks**: If you're unsure of your exact location, note any nearby landmarks or street names to help emergency services find you faster.

- **Document Copies**: Carry a photocopy of your passport and keep digital backups of important documents to simplify things in case of loss or theft.

10.0 TRAVEL TIPS

10.1 BEST TIME TO VISIT

Nuremberg's charm is timeless, but the best time to visit depends on the experience you're after. Each season here has its own appeal, from lively festivals and sunlit beer gardens to cozy winter markets. Here's a guide to help you pick the perfect time for your visit.

Spring (March to May)

Spring in Nuremberg is a season of renewal, with blooming flowers and mild temperatures that steadily warm as the months progress. This is an ideal time for exploring Nuremberg's Old Town, strolling through Tiergarten Park, or enjoying a river cruise on the Pegnitz. Temperatures range from 5°C to 18°C (41°F to 64°F) and, while rain showers are common, they're usually brief.

In April, Nuremberg's Volksfest kicks off, filling the city with carnival rides, beer tents, and traditional Bavarian cuisine. It's a more local and relaxed alternative to Oktoberfest but equally festive. If you're seeking a lively atmosphere without the summer crowds, spring is a fantastic time to visit.

Highlights:

- Spring blooms in Nuremberg's parks and gardens

- Fewer tourists compared to summer

- Nuremberg Volksfest (April)

Summer (June to August)

Summer is the high season in Nuremberg, with warm days, long evenings, and a full calendar of outdoor events. Temperatures average between 13°C and 25°C (55°F to 77°F), making it ideal for wandering the Old Town, exploring Nuremberg Castle, or enjoying the city's outdoor beer gardens.

One of summer's main highlights is the Nuremberg Bardentreffen, a free world music festival held in late July, where over 200 acts perform on stages across the city. The Blue Night (Blaue Nacht) also takes place in May, transforming the Old Town into a mesmerizing light show with art installations.

However, keep in mind that this is Nuremberg's busiest season. If you're visiting during summer, consider booking accommodations well in advance to secure your preferred options.

Highlights:

- Warm weather and extended daylight hours

- Bardentreffen Music Festival (July)

- Lively beer gardens and riverside activities

Autumn (September to November)

Autumn is a delightful season to visit Nuremberg as the city is bathed in hues of gold and crimson. Temperatures in September are still warm, averaging 10°C to 20°C (50°F to 68°F), and the early part of autumn is less crowded than summer, making it a great time to explore.

This is also a season of festivals, including the Nuremberg Fall Festival (Herbstvolksfest), a smaller counterpart to Munich's Oktoberfest that runs from late August to mid-September. Oktoberfest in nearby Munich draws crowds, but Nuremberg's celebration offers a more intimate

Bavarian experience with rides, food stalls, and, of course, plenty of beer.

October and November bring cooler weather, but it's an atmospheric time to stroll the medieval streets and admire the changing leaves in the city's parks.

Highlights:

- Mild weather and fewer tourists

- Nuremberg Fall Festival (August - September)

- Beautiful autumn foliage

Winter (December to February)

Winter in Nuremberg is synonymous with the iconic Christkindlesmarkt, one of the most famous Christmas markets in the world. Held from late November to December, this festive market transforms the city's Hauptmarkt into a winter wonderland with wooden stalls, mulled wine, gingerbread, and hand-crafted gifts. The Christkindlesmarkt draws thousands, so be prepared for crowds if visiting during this period.

The coldest months are January and February, with temperatures ranging from -2°C to 5°C (28°F to 41°F). However, the quiet post-holiday season offers a more tranquil experience, and Nuremberg's cozy cafes and historic museums are perfect for indoor exploration.

Highlights:

- Christkindlesmarkt (late November - December)

- Romantic winter ambiance in the Old Town

- Quiet museums and cultural sites in January and February

Overall Best Time to Visit

For pleasant weather and a range of activities, **spring and autumn** offer a balanced experience with moderate crowds, mild temperatures, and a range of local events. However, if your heart is set on experiencing Nuremberg's legendary Christmas market, winter is the season for you.

10.2 NAVIGATING THE CITY

Navigating Nuremberg is a seamless experience, thanks to its efficient transportation network, well-marked signage, and pedestrian-friendly layout. Here's a complete guide to getting around, whether you prefer public transit, walking, or cycling.

1. Public Transportation: Nuremberg's VAG Network

Nuremberg's VAG (Verkehrs-Aktiengesellschaft Nürnberg) operates an extensive and reliable public transportation system. It includes:

- **U-Bahn (Subway)**: The U-Bahn has four main lines (U1, U2, U3, and U11) that connect most major attractions, neighborhoods, and shopping areas.

U-Bahn stations are well-signed, and trains arrive frequently, especially during peak hours.

- **S-Bahn (Suburban Train)**: For trips beyond the city center or to nearby towns, the S-Bahn is ideal. Lines like S1 connect to areas such as Fürth and Erlangen, while others reach scenic spots in the surrounding Franconian countryside.

- **Trams and Buses**: The tram system serves neighborhoods where U-Bahn and S-Bahn lines don't reach, while buses cover nearly every corner of the city. Trams offer a scenic way to explore Nuremberg and have convenient stops near major tourist sites.

- **Ticketing**: VAG offers single tickets, day passes, and multi-day options. For tourists, the Nuremberg Card offers free travel on all public transportation and free or discounted entry to many attractions.

- **Ticket Zones and Validity**: Nuremberg's public transport operates within different zones, but most tourist areas fall under Zone A. Tickets can be purchased from machines at stations, through the VAG app, or on some buses directly from the driver.

2. Biking Around Nuremberg

Cycling is popular in Nuremberg, and the city has developed bike lanes on most major streets.

- **Bike Rentals**: Several rental services, such as Nextbike, offer bikes that can be rented for short-term use. Bike-sharing stations are conveniently located near major landmarks and transit hubs.

- **Popular Bike Routes**: The city's Old Town is highly walkable and bike-friendly, and exploring by bike is ideal for scenic routes along the Pegnitz River. The Ringpark around the Old Town's medieval walls is a particularly enjoyable area for cyclists.

- **Tips**: Be cautious on cobblestone streets, especially in the Altstadt (Old Town), and always lock your bike securely when parking.

3. Exploring on Foot

Walking is one of the best ways to experience Nuremberg's charm. The Old Town, or Altstadt, is compact and pedestrian-friendly, with historic sites close together, making it easy to explore by foot.

- **Pedestrian Zones**: The city center has several pedestrian-only areas, including Hauptmarkt, where you'll find the famous Frauenkirche and Schöner Brunnen. Many smaller streets in the Altstadt also restrict vehicle traffic, creating a pleasant, car-free atmosphere for tourists.

- **Sightseeing on Foot**: Starting from the Kaiserburg Castle, visitors can stroll through the medieval lanes, past Albrecht Dürer's House, to the vibrant shopping streets around Karolinenstraße. Nuremberg's signage helps guide you between key sites, and many streets are lined with markers that tell the story of the city's rich history.

4. Taxi and Ride-Sharing Options

Taxis in Nuremberg are plentiful and convenient but are typically more expensive than public transport. They are available at major hubs like the main train station (Hauptbahnhof) and the airport, as well as at dedicated taxi ranks across the city.

- **Ride-Sharing**: Services like Uber and Free Now are also available in Nuremberg, providing more flexibility and often cheaper fares than traditional taxis.

- **Tips**: If you're staying outside the city center or planning to travel late at night, these services can be a practical option.

5. Driving and Car Rentals

If you plan to explore beyond Nuremberg, renting a car can be beneficial, but driving within the city isn't always recommended due to narrow streets, one-way systems, and limited parking, especially in the Altstadt.

- **Parking**: Public parking garages are available throughout the city center, with fees that vary based on location and time of day. Additionally, the city has Park & Ride options near transit hubs, which let visitors park outside the center and take public transport to avoid congestion.

- **Eco-Friendly Driving**: Nuremberg, like many German cities, has established low-emission zones. If you're renting a car, ensure it has the necessary emissions sticker, or you may incur fines.

6. Useful Tips for Tourists

- **City Map and Apps**: Pick up a city map from the tourist information centers at Hauptbahnhof or online. The VAG app is also helpful for checking schedules and finding the best routes in real time.

- **Language**: While signage is often in German, many public transport maps and ticket machines have English options, and station staff are generally helpful in providing assistance.

- **Safety**: Nuremberg is a safe city, and its transport system is generally well-monitored. Still, it's best to be cautious with personal belongings, especially in crowded areas like Hauptmarkt.

10.3 CULTURAL ETIQUETTE

When visiting Nuremberg, understanding and respecting local customs can greatly enhance your experience. The city, with its rich history, is a place where tradition and modernity intertwine, and locals take pride in their culture and heritage. Here's a guide to the key cultural etiquette that will help you navigate your time in Nuremberg with ease.

1. Greetings and Addressing People

In Nuremberg, as throughout Germany, greetings are an important part of daily life. A firm handshake is the most common form of greeting, especially in business settings. When meeting someone for the first time, it's polite to make eye contact and offer a handshake. In more casual or family settings, hugs or cheek kisses are common once a relationship has been established, though this is typically reserved for close friends or family members.

When addressing people, it's customary to use formal titles (Herr for Mr. and Frau for Mrs.), followed by the person's last name unless they specifically tell you to use their first name. Using "Sie" (the formal 'you') is expected in professional or unfamiliar settings, while "du" (the informal 'you') is used among close friends or younger people, but only once you've been invited to do so.

2. Punctuality

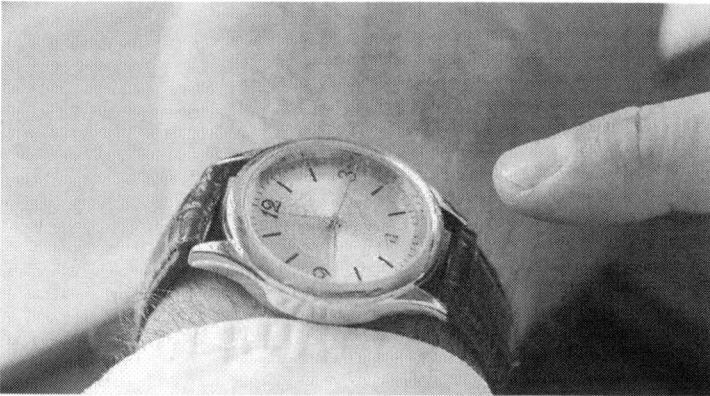

Germans value punctuality, and Nuremberg is no exception. Arriving on time for meetings, dinners, and appointments is considered a sign of respect. If you're running late, it's courteous to call ahead and inform the host or party. For social gatherings, arriving within 10-15 minutes of the designated time is typical, though it's never appropriate to arrive too early, as this may put undue pressure on your host.

3. Dining Etiquette

Dining in Nuremberg follows traditional German table manners. When sitting at the table, it's polite to wait for the host to begin the meal. German meals typically involve a variety of courses, and it's important to follow the flow of the meal.

- **Utensils**: Germans use their utensils properly: forks in the left hand and knives in the right. Never switch hands while eating.

- **Clinking Glasses**: When toasting, it's customary to make eye contact with the person you're clinking glasses with. Germans are very particular about this small gesture. A simple "Prost!" (cheers) is said before taking a drink, whether it's beer, wine, or any other beverage.

- **Tipping**: Tipping is customary in Nuremberg, with 5-10% being the typical range for good service in restaurants. Tipping in taxis, hotels, and cafes is also appreciated but not mandatory. It's polite to hand the tip directly to the waiter rather than leaving it on the table.

4. Personal Space and Politeness

Personal space is important in Nuremberg, and Germans generally value their privacy. Public spaces are usually quiet, with people respecting one another's personal space in elevators, on public transport, and in lines. When speaking, Germans tend to be direct but not rude. If you're asked a question, a thoughtful and clear answer is appreciated.

While it's okay to engage in small talk with strangers in certain settings, don't expect people to open up immediately. Germans are often more reserved when it comes to personal matters, especially with people they don't know well.

5. Public Behavior and Quietness

In Nuremberg, and Germany in general, public behavior is often characterized by a sense of order and quietness. Speaking loudly, especially on public transportation, is frowned upon. People generally keep their voices low in public areas, and being overly animated or loud may be seen as disruptive or inconsiderate. In restaurants and cafes, it's also common for people to keep their conversations at a moderate level to maintain a calm atmosphere.

441

6. Dress Code

The dress code in Nuremberg tends to be smart and conservative, especially in business settings. While casual attire is acceptable for most tourist attractions, you'll find that locals tend to dress neatly and with care. When visiting churches or formal events, it's best to dress modestly and appropriately. In winter, be prepared for cold weather—warm coats, scarves, and gloves are essential, while summer calls for breathable fabrics and comfortable shoes for walking.

7. Environmental Awareness

Germany, and Nuremberg in particular, is known for its strong commitment to sustainability and environmental awareness. Locals take pride in recycling and conserving resources. You'll find clearly marked bins for paper, plastics, and organic waste in most public areas. When visiting local markets, consider bringing your own reusable shopping bags. Also, if you are staying in a hotel or using public transportation, be mindful of energy-saving practices, such as turning off lights when leaving a room and conserving water.

8. Respect for History

Nuremberg is a city rich in historical significance, from its medieval landmarks to its role in the history of World War II. When visiting historical sites such as the Nuremberg Trials Memorial, it's important to approach these places with respect and understanding. Many locals have a deep sense of responsibility to remember history, and visiting these sites should be done with reverence and respect for the solemn nature of the events they commemorate.

9. Holidays and Festivals

Nuremberg is known for its vibrant festivals, especially around Christmas. The Nuremberg Christkindlesmarkt (Christmas market) is one of the most famous in Germany. If you plan to visit during the holidays, it's important to recognize that the city takes its holiday traditions seriously, and locals may have special customs related to family gatherings, gifts, and meals.

During events and festivals, it's polite to join in the festivities but also observe local customs. For example, at the Christmas market, it's common to sample traditional foods such as Nuremberg bratwurst and mulled wine. If invited to a local home for a holiday or celebration, it's customary to bring a small gift, such as flowers, wine, or chocolates, to express gratitude.

10. Language

While many people in Nuremberg speak English, especially in tourist areas, learning a few basic German phrases can go a long way in showing respect for the local culture. Simple greetings like "Guten Morgen" (Good morning), "Danke" (Thank you), and "Tschüss" (Goodbye) will be appreciated. Making an effort to speak German, even if it's just a few words, can endear you to locals and enhance your travel experience.

10.4 USEFUL APPS AND RESOURCES

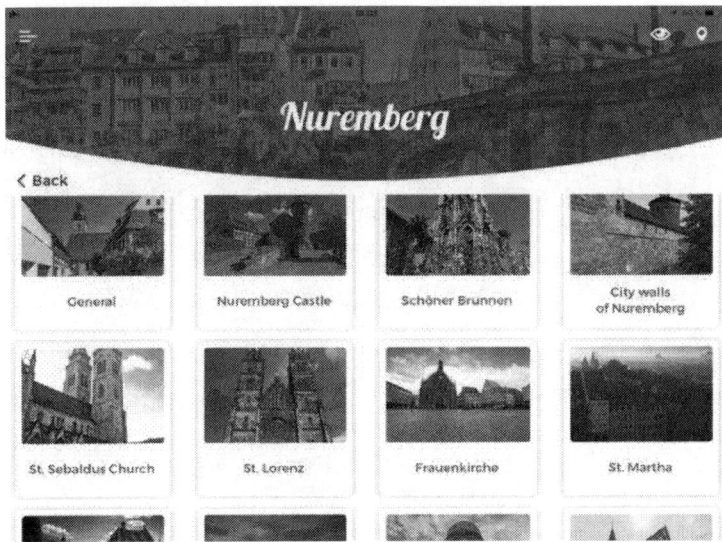

When visiting Nuremberg, having the right tools at your fingertips can greatly enhance your experience. From navigation to local insights, here are some essential apps and resources to help you navigate the city with ease and make the most of your trip.

1. Public Transport Apps

VAG Fahrinfo

The VAG Fahrinfo app is essential for getting around Nuremberg using public transportation. It provides real-time updates on buses, trams, and the U-Bahn, allowing you to plan your journey, check timetables, and track departures. It also allows you to buy tickets directly within the app, making your travel experience more convenient.

DB Navigator

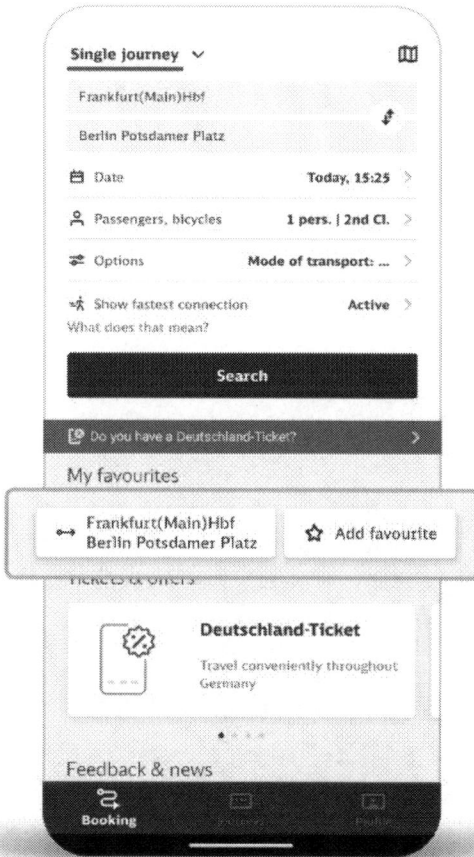

For train travel to and from Nuremberg, DB Navigator is a must-have. This app from Deutsche Bahn (DB) offers train schedules, real-time updates, and mobile ticketing for both local and long-distance trains. It's helpful if you're planning day trips to nearby cities or exploring Germany by rail.

2. Tourism and City Guides

Nuremberg Tourism App

Official tourism apps, like the Nuremberg Tourism app, provide helpful information on key attractions, events, and local tips. It offers detailed descriptions of sights such as Nuremberg Castle, the Albrecht Dürer House, and the Germanisches Nationalmuseum, along with interactive maps and recommended itineraries.

TripAdvisor

For general reviews and recommendations, TripAdvisor can be indispensable. Search for local restaurants, museums, and tours, and read up on fellow travelers' experiences to make informed decisions. TripAdvisor is especially useful for finding hidden gems and local favorites in Nuremberg.

3. Dining and Food Delivery

HappyCow

●●●○○ Sprint 🛜   8:46 AM   ✈ ❷ ✳ 54% 🔋⚡

Help!   🐮 **HappyCow**

All Listings   ›

Ⓥ   Vegan Only   ›

🍃   Vegetarian Only   ›

🤲   Vegetarian Friendly   ›

🏪   Stores + More   ›

Nearby   Search   Favorites   Trips

455

Whether you're a vegan, vegetarian, or simply looking for healthy dining options, HappyCow is an app to have on hand. It helps you find plant-based restaurants, cafes, and eateries in Nuremberg, complete with reviews and menus. It's especially helpful in a city with a growing food scene catering to diverse tastes.

Uber Eats

If you're craving food from the comfort of your accommodation, Uber Eats makes it easy to order food from a wide variety of local restaurants. Whether it's a quick snack or a multi-course meal, this app brings the local flavors straight to your door.

4. Language and Communication

Google Translate

While many people in Nuremberg speak English, it's always useful to have a language translation app on hand, especially if you're venturing off the beaten path. Google Translate can help you navigate menus, signs, or engage with locals more confidently by translating text or speech in real-time.

Duolingo

If you're planning to learn a bit of German before your trip, Duolingo is a fun and effective way to practice key phrases and vocabulary. Even learning basic greetings and expressions can go a long way in making connections with the locals.

5. Navigation and Maps

Google Maps

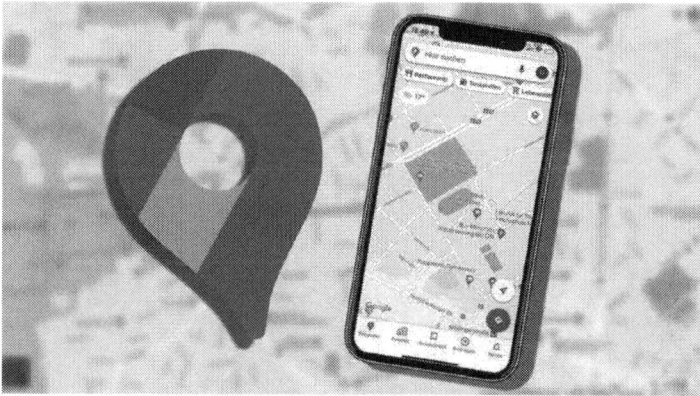

One of the most reliable apps for navigating Nuremberg, Google Maps provides turn-by-turn navigation, public transport options, and walking routes. It also highlights points of interest, including museums, parks, and historical sites, making it a go-to app for any traveler.

Maps.me

If you don't have access to data while traveling, Maps.me is a great alternative. It allows you to download offline maps of Nuremberg and provides detailed walking routes and tourist attractions. It's perfect for use in areas with limited mobile service.

6. Local Events and Attractions

Eventbrite

For travelers seeking cultural events, concerts, and local experiences, Eventbrite can help you discover happenings in Nuremberg. From art exhibitions to outdoor festivals, this app provides a curated list of events along with booking options, so you never miss out on exciting activities.

GetYourGuide

Whether you're booking a guided tour of the Nuremberg Castle or a special event like the famous Christkindlesmarkt, GetYourGuide is the app for tickets and tours. You can book tickets for museums, sightseeing tours, and other experiences in advance, often skipping the long queues.

7. Currency and Budgeting

XE Currency

For international travelers, XE Currency is an invaluable app for checking exchange rates and converting currencies. It provides live exchange rate data and allows you to calculate conversions between your home currency and euros, helping you manage your budget while traveling.

Revolut

If you want to avoid hefty bank fees while traveling abroad, consider using Revolut. This app allows you to transfer money, check exchange rates, and withdraw cash at ATMs in Nuremberg, all while offering competitive exchange rates.

8. Emergency and Health

MyTrips

This app helps you keep track of your flight details, hotel bookings, and transportation schedules all in one place. It's especially helpful if you have multiple bookings or need reminders for time-sensitive activities. Having everything organized ensures you won't miss important travel details while in Nuremberg.

DoctorBox

In case of a medical emergency, DoctorBox is an app that can help you find nearby medical facilities, pharmacies, and emergency services. It's always a good idea to be prepared, especially when traveling in a foreign country.

9. Travel Communities

Couchsurfing

For travelers interested in meeting locals, Couchsurfing is a great way to connect with people who may be willing to offer a place to stay or show you around Nuremberg. It's also a social app, allowing you to find meetups or local events while exploring the city.

Meetup

If you want to engage with like-minded travelers or locals, Meetup is a great platform to join events or activities in Nuremberg. Whether it's a group hike, a language exchange, or a social gathering, Meetup offers a wide variety of activities to help you connect with others.

11.0 CONCLUSION

11.1 FINAL THOUGHTS ON NUREMBERG

Nuremberg is a city that effortlessly bridges the gap between its historic past and its vibrant present. From its iconic medieval architecture and the formidable Kaiserburg Castle to its buzzing contemporary art scene and world-class museums, Nuremberg is a destination that has something for everyone. It's a place where history comes alive, where cobblestone streets whisper stories of centuries gone by, and where every corner has its own unique tale to tell.

For history enthusiasts, Nuremberg offers unparalleled opportunities to delve into the narratives that shaped Europe—from the grandeur of the Holy Roman Empire to the sobering lessons of the 20th century. At the same time, its modern pulse, reflected in bustling markets, innovative culinary experiences, and thriving cultural events, ensures that visitors leave with a sense of the city's dynamic present.

Nuremberg is not just a city to visit; it's a city to experience. Whether you're savoring a freshly grilled bratwurst at the Hauptmarkt, marveling at the craftsmanship of local artisans, or exploring the charming neighborhoods along the Pegnitz River, the city invites you to slow down and truly immerse yourself.

Practicality also sets Nuremberg apart. Its excellent transportation network makes it easy to explore both the city and the surrounding Franconian countryside. Whether it's a day trip to Bamberg or Rothenburg ob der Tauber, or simply a scenic train ride through the region, Nuremberg serves as a perfect base for deeper explorations.

As you prepare to leave, the memory of Nuremberg lingers—a warm mix of medieval charm, cultural depth, and modern flair. It's a city that leaves an indelible mark, encouraging you to return and uncover even more of its treasures. Whether it's your first visit or one of many, Nuremberg never stops surprising, inspiring, and captivating.

Nuremberg isn't just a destination—it's a journey through time, taste, and tradition. May your visit leave you with cherished memories, broadened perspectives, and a longing to explore further.

Safe travels and see you again in Nuremberg!

11.2 ENCOURAGEMENT TO EXPLORE

Nuremberg is more than just a city; it's a tapestry of history, culture, and charm waiting to be unraveled. For travelers, it presents a rare opportunity to step into a vibrant blend of medieval allure and modern vitality. Whether you're wandering through its cobblestone streets or gazing at its stunning skyline dominated by the imperial castle, Nuremberg invites you to explore at every turn.

A Journey Through Time

One of the most enchanting aspects of Nuremberg is its ability to transport you through centuries of history. As you walk along the city walls or stand in the shadows of Albrecht Dürer's house, you're tracing steps that echo the stories of emperors, artists, and revolutionaries. The city's museums, such as the Germanisches Nationalmuseum, offer an immersive dive into the Middle Ages, while landmarks like the Kaiserburg Castle and St. Lorenz Church showcase the grandeur of a bygone era.

Beyond the Old Town

While Nuremberg's Altstadt (Old Town) is undoubtedly its heart, there's so much more to discover. Venture into the districts surrounding the historic core to experience a different rhythm of life. The trendy Gostenhof neighborhood buzzes with creativity, offering an eclectic mix of galleries, cafes, and boutique shops. Meanwhile, the serene Pegnitz River meanders through the city, providing idyllic spots for relaxation or leisurely walks.

The Culinary Adventure

Exploration doesn't stop at landmarks—it extends to your palate. Nuremberg is a haven for food lovers, renowned for its iconic Nürnberger Rostbratwurst and Lebkuchen (gingerbread). From traditional Franconian restaurants to bustling markets and modern eateries, every meal is an invitation to savor the flavors of the region.

Festivals and Experiences

No matter the season, Nuremberg has a way of making you feel part of its story. Visit during the world-famous Christkindlesmarkt to experience a magical holiday tradition, or enjoy the summertime vibes at the Bardentreffen music festival. Each event and celebration offers a unique insight into the city's vibrant culture.

Embrace Spontaneity

Some of the most rewarding travel moments come when you let go of the itinerary and allow curiosity to lead the way. Take a detour, peek into a hidden courtyard, or strike up a conversation with a local. In Nuremberg, every street and encounter has the potential to surprise and delight.

Your Adventure Awaits

Nuremberg invites you not just to visit, but to immerse yourself in its story. Let its beauty, culture, and spirit inspire you to explore deeper, wander farther, and create unforgettable memories. Whether it's your first visit or a return trip, Nuremberg promises an adventure that stays with you long after you leave.

Printed in Great Britain
by Amazon